THE OFFICIAL GUIDE TO
Grand Canyon's North Rim

STEWART AITCHISON

GRAND CANYON
CONSERVANCY

GRAND CANYON
CONSERVANCY

P.O. Box 399, Grand Canyon, AZ 86023
(800) 858-2808 grandcanyon.org

Composed in the United States of America
Printed in the United States of America

Fourth Edition 2020
24 23 22 21 20   1 2 3 4 5

ISBN 978-1-934656-99-0

Edited by Claudine Taillac and Susan Tasaki
Designed by David Jenney Design

CONTENTS

Welcome to the North Rim

There is much to love about the North Rim of the Grand Canyon at the southernmost extent of the Kaibab Plateau, including the experience of traveling through one of the most enchanting forests in the American Southwest to reach it. Even without the added bonus of the great gorge, the Kaibab Plateau is worth a visit.

The North Rim is also the quiet side of the canyon. Nearly six million people visit the South Rim each year, but only one-tenth that number make it to the "other side." Its remoteness is one of several reasons for these lower numbers—it's out of the way. Travelers along Interstate 40 often make the short detour up to the South Rim for a quick look at the canyon, but the North Rim is off the beaten path; it takes extra planning to get there, and there are few accommodations. Winter also limits visitation, as the highway leading into the park is closed for nearly half the year—from approximately late November until mid-May—by deep snow.

However, the extra effort offers opportunities to visit other national parks and public lands relatively close to the North Rim (and to each other) as well. While these areas are scenically different from one another, they're complementary in terms of geological and biological attributes.

This corner of the geological wonderland called the Colorado Plateau is a special part of North America's Southwest. It's big place. Take your time, stop often, and enjoy a part of America that has changed little over the years.

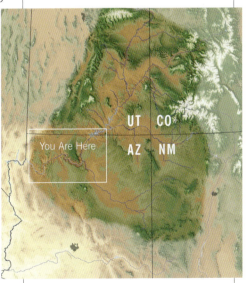

The Grand Canyon lies within the Colorado Plateau, which spans the Four Corners region.

Plan Your Visit

GETTING THERE

No matter from which direction you approach the North Rim of the Grand Canyon, you must navigate part of the Arizona Strip, the area north of the Grand Canyon and south of the Utah/Arizona border—nearly five million acres of the emptiest territory in the lower forty-eight. The park can only be accessed by motorized vehicles and bicycles, and its remote location calls for advance trip planning; reservations are recommended for accommodations, both within the park and in the small towns en route. The closest airport is approximately two hours away.

Section Three of this book provides detailed information about approaches and attractions, and on the inside back cover, you'll find a map to help you plan your route.

THE NORTH RIM ENTRANCE STATION

The entrance to Grand Canyon National Park's North Rim is 30 miles (48 km) south of Jacob Lake on Highway 67, and the actual rim of the Grand Canyon is an additional 14 miles (23 km) south of the entrance. The town of Jacob Lake is located in northern Arizona on Highway 89A, not far from the Utah border. Grand Canyon National Park itself lies entirely within the state of Arizona.

As you approach the North Rim from Jacob Lake, you will pass through a long, narrow meadow lined with a boreal forest of Engelmann spruce, alpine and white firs, Douglas-fir, and aspen. In the meadow are mountain muhly, blue grama, and squirrel-tail grasses along with lupine, yarrow, and aster.

It's a great place to see mule deer or bison during early mornings or late afternoons, or an occasional coyote stalking gophers or voles. The nearby forest is home to blue grouse, rare three-toed woodpeckers, ruby-crowned kinglets, and Clark's nutcrackers.

The park road meanders south through Thompson Canyon to an intersection with Fuller Canyon, where a side road leads to viewpoints on the Walhalla

Plateau. This part of the Kaibab Plateau was named by cartographer François Emile Matthes in 1904 for the great hall of the Scandinavian gods, but local cowboys called it Greenland Plateau.

Continue south on the main park road to the Bright Angel Point area, where the National Park Service Visitor Center and Grand Canyon Lodge are located.

SERVICES AND FACILITIES INSIDE THE PARK

Open mid-May to mid-October.
See map on inside front cover for locations. Visit: nps.gov/grca/planyourvisit/north-rim.htm

The Visitor Center, built in a style known as National Park Service rustic.

NPS North Rim Visitor Center

▶ Information, interpretive exhibits, park ranger programs, drinking water, bathrooms.

Grand Canyon Conservancy Park Store

▶ Books, gifts, passport stamp: grandcanyon.org

NPS Backcountry Information Center/Permit Office

▶ Backcountry hikes information, overnight backcountry permits, hiking maps, drinking water, bathrooms.
▶ Visit: nps.gov/grca/planyourvisit/backcountry-permit.htm

NPS Campground

▶ Water refill and dump stations, no hookups.
▶ Reservations required: recreation.gov or (877) 444-6777.

Grand Canyon Lodge

▶ Accommodations include lodge rooms and cabins.
▶ Visit: nps.gov/grca/planyourvisit/lodging-nr.htm

Dining at Grand Canyon Lodge

There are several options for dining at the lodge.

▶ The dining room, with its sweeping views of the canyon, serves breakfast, lunch, and dinner (reservations are recommended for dinner).
▶ For a quick breakfast, lunch, or dinner, the Deli in the Pines is an excellent option, and is also a good place for hikers to provision themselves with trail snacks.
▶ Visitors often begin their day with coffee and fresh baked-goods from the Coffee Shop and enjoy post-hike cold beverages and snacks in the Roughrider Saloon.

The Sunroom at Grand Canyon Lodge provides a magnificent panoramic view.

General Store

Originally the Grand Canyon Inn (built in 1929), the store is stocked with groceries, camping supplies.

▶ ATM and wi-fi are available.

Gas Station

▶ 24-hour pay-at-the-pump, gas and diesel available.

Canyon Trail Rides

▶ One-hour mule rides along the rim, half-day rides along the rim, and trips down into Grand Canyon are usually available.
▶ Register at the Canyon Trail Rides desk in the lodge lobby.

SERVICES AND FACILITIES OUTSIDE THE PARK

Lodging, camping, food, and services north of the park on Highway 67

Kaibab Lodge

Located 18 miles (29 km) north of the North Rim Visitor Center.

▶ Open mid-May to mid-October.
▶ Lodging and restaurant. Reservations: kaibablodge.com or (928) 638-2389.

DeMotte Campground

U.S. Forest Service campground, 18 miles (29 km) north of the North Rim Visitor Center.

▶ Open mid-May to mid-October.
▶ Reservations: recreation.gov or (877) 444-6777.

North Rim Country Store

Located 18 miles (29 km) north of the North Rim Visitor Center.

▶ Open mid-May to mid-October.
▶ Convenience store, gas station, tire repair, propane, and ATM. (928) 638-2383.

Kaibab Plateau Visitor Center

Jacob Lake, Arizona, 45 miles (72 km) north of the North Rim Visitor Center.

▶ Open mid-May to mid-October.
▶ Information and a Grand Canyon Conservancy Park Store with books, maps, and gifts; (928) 643-7298.

Jacob Lake Inn

Jacob Lake, Arizona, 45 miles (72 km) north of the North Rim Visitor Center.

▶ Open year-round.
▶ Restaurant, gift shop, propane, and gas station with 24 hour pay-at-the-pump.
▶ Reservations: jacoblake.com or (928) 643-7232.

Kaibab Camper Village

Private campground, 0.25 miles (0.5 km) south of Jacob Lake on Forest Service Road 461 off Highway 67.

▶ Open mid-May to mid-October.
▶ Reservations: kaibabcampervillage. com or (928) 643-7804.

Jacob Lake Campground

U.S. Forest Service campground, 45 miles (72 km) north of the North Rim Visitor Center.

▶ Open mid-May to mid-October.
▶ Reservations: recreation.gov or (877) 444-6777.

SAFETY

▶ Watch out for wildlife on the roads, particularly mule deer, bison, and turkeys.
▶ Do not approach or feed wildlife; that cute squirrel may bite, and its fleas may transmit plague. It's illegal to feed wildlife in national parks.
▶ Avoid exposed rims and solitary trees during thunderstorms. If you can hear thunder, lightning is close enough to strike you.
▶ Drink plenty of water; it's easy to become dehydrated.
▶ Take it slowly; you are at high elevation, which taxes the body to the extreme.
▶ If you decide to explore off the main paved highways, go prepared. Have a full tank of gas and take plenty of

food and water.
- ► Cell phone reception is spotty at best.
- ► GPS units have been known to lead visitors astray and into serious trouble. Know how to read a map, and use common sense. Tell someone where you are going and when you plan to return.
- ► Remember that secondary roads can become impassable after rain or snow storms.

LEAVE NO TRACE

The ethic for exploring forests, parks, and wild areas, its basic principles include:
- ► Plan ahead and prepare.
- ► Travel and camp on durable surfaces.
- ► Dispose of waste properly.
- ► Leave what you find.
- ► If campfires are allowed, minimize their impact.
- ► Respect wildlife.
- ► Be courteous to other visitors.

A PLACE OF EXTREMES

- ► At the Bright Angel Ranger Station on the North Rim, a frigid winter low of -22°F (-30°C) has been recorded.
- ► At Phantom Ranch near the Colorado River—fewer than eight miles away—summer temperatures can soar to a scorching 120°F (49°C) or more.
- ► The North Rim averages 26 inches (66 cm) of precipitation annually, and about half of that comes in the form of snow: 142 inches (360 cm) on average per year, with a record snowfall of 272 inches (691 cm) in 1978.
- ► The South Rim, a good 1,000 feet lower than the North Rim, averages only 58 inches (147 cm) of snow.
- ► Phantom Ranch receives less than 1 inch (2.5 cm) of snow annually.
- ► Lees Ferry, the driest part of the Arizona Strip, averages only 6.1 inches (15.5 cm) of rain per year.

Average Temperatures at the North Rim

	JAN	FEB	MAR	APR	MAY	JUN	JUL	AUG	SEP	OCT	NOV	DEC
High (F)	37	39	44	53	62	73	77	75	69	59	46	40
Low (F)	16	18	21	29	34	40	46	45	39	31	24	20
High (C)	3	4	7	12	17	23	25	24	21	15	8	4
Low (C)	-9	-8	-6	-2	1	4	8	7	4	-1	-4	-7

Average Precipitation in Inches at Grand Canyon

	JAN	FEB	MAR	APR	MAY	JUN	JUL	AUG	SEP	OCT	NOV	DEC
North Rim	3.17	3.22	2.65	1.73	1.17	0.86	1.93	2.85	1.99	1.38	1.48	2.83
South Rim	1.32	1.55	1.38	0.93	0.66	0.42	1.81	2.25	1.56	1.10	0.94	1.64
Inner Canyon	0.68	0.75	0.79	0.47	0.36	0.30	0.84	1.40	0.97	0.65	0.43	0.87

Point Imperial

A SPECIAL NOTE ABOUT WINTER VISITS

Visiting the North Rim during the winter is a serious undertaking. Arizona Highway 67 from Jacob Lake to the park entrance is closed in the winter due to snow, which means that it's about a 31-mile (50-km) ski/snowshoe trek or snowmobile ride just to reach the park boundary.

▶ No motorized vehicles are allowed in the park during the winter.

▶ Traversing any of the icy trails may require crampons and ice axes or hiking poles.

Contact the NPS Backcountry Information Center before even considering such an expedition.

LAND MANAGEMENT AGENCIES

Various federal agencies manage the land in this corner of the country.

On American Indian reservations, which are sovereign entities or territories, the Bureau of Indian Affairs (BIA), part of the Department of the Interior, administers federal programs. Most reservations also have their own tribal government and elected officials.

National parks, national monuments, and national recreation areas are usually managed by the National Park Service (NPS), also under the Department of the Interior. Parks and recreation areas are designated by Congress, whereas monuments are established by presidential proclamation. Some of the newer monuments on the Arizona Strip were created out of Bureau of Land Management (BLM) land (the BLM is another subdivision of the Department of the Interior) and are managed jointly by the BLM and the NPS. Kaibab National

Forest is managed by the U.S. Forest Service (USFS), which is part of the Department of Agriculture. Finally, there are congressionally designated wilderness areas, which can be within any of the above areas (except the reservations).

Each type of land has its own rules and regulations, so to stay out of trouble, be sure to contact the appropriate agency. *See the appendix for contact information.*

DISPERSED CAMPING

You may camp independently (away from campgrounds) in the Kaibab National Forest. Stop at the Kaibab Plateau Visitor Center in Jacob Lake, Arizona, for information.

► No garbage service; pack out what you take in.
► Bring water; few reliable water sources exist.
► Camp at least 0.25 mile (0.4 km) from water sources to allow access for wildlife and livestock.
► Check fire restrictions and be fire-safe (carry a shovel and bucket).
► Bury human waste at least 6 inches (15 cm) deep and 100 feet (30 m) from water sources and drainage.

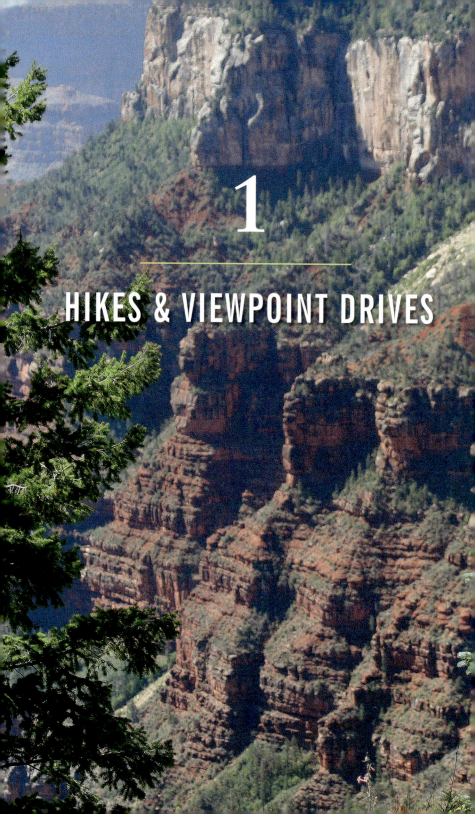

1

HIKES & VIEWPOINT DRIVES

Northwest Area

The trails included here are shown on the NPS Pocket Map, which the National Park Service provides upon entering the park (maps are also available at the North Rim Visitor Center). Other commercial Grand Canyon maps show additional old trails on the North Rim, which are neither signed nor maintained. Check with the NPS Backcountry Information Center/Permit Office for current camping, hiking, and backpacking regulations concerning these routes. Wear appropriate clothing and head gear, and carry water, sunscreen, and food with you on all North Rim hikes.

1 Bright Angel Point Trail

DISTANCE: 0.5 miles (0.8 km) round trip; allow 30 minutes.
DIFFICULTY: Easy with a few steep sections; mostly paved.
WATER: None.

Begin at the log shelter in the parking area near the North Rim Visitor Center, or from the back porch of the Grand Canyon Lodge.

If taken in the evening, this short, quarter-mile (0.4 km) stroll from the Grand Canyon Lodge to Bright Angel Point (8,148 feet/2,484 meters above sea level) reveals views enhanced by the waning light. The trail runs along a knife-edged ridge separating Roaring Springs Canyon and The Transept. Powell named the hidden creek below "Bright Angel" after a character in Milton's *Paradise Lost*, to contrast with a muddy stream in Utah that he had christened Dirty Devil.

> *"The view from Bright Angel proved fully up to recollection and expectation as affording an intimate panorama of the buttes, temples, and towers in the most crowded and characteristic part of the Kaibab division of the canyon."*
> —GEORGE FRASER, TOURIST, 1916

Listen for the rush of water far below at Roaring Springs. This large spring provides all the potable water for both the North and South Rims. At dusk, the secret inner canyon is already in deep shadow. Deva, Brahma, and Zoroaster Temples, all named by early U.S. Geological Survey geologist Clarence Dutton, glow in the decreasing light, and far to the south, the San Francisco Peaks oversee a phalanx of lesser

View from Bright Angel Point.

volcanoes, some 600 in number. While it is only 10 miles (16 km) as the raven flies to Grand Canyon Village on the South Rim, by trail, the distance is 22 miles (35 km), and by road, it is more than 200 miles (322 km) away.

Silk-tassel bush, piñons, gnarled junipers, and Gambel oak grow along the trail. The Kaibab Limestone is spotted with chert nodules, crinoid stems, pieces of shell, and colorful lichens.

2 Transept Trail

DISTANCE: 2 miles (3.2 km) one-way; allow 1 hour.
DIFFICULTY: Moderate; dirt and gravel surface.
WATER: None.

This pleasant walk through an old-growth ponderosa pine forest with canyon views starts at Grand Canyon Lodge, skirts along the rim of The Transept, and ends past the campground, where it intersects with the Bridle Path.

Geologist Clarence Dutton, who named The Transept in 1882, considered it "far grander than Yosemite." Comparing one of the most beautiful places on Earth to another of the most beautiful places on Earth only serves to emphasize the profound beauty to be encountered on this short, two-mile journey.

In a minimal distance, the trail showcases the vast diversity of the relationship between the Kaibab Plateau and the Grand Canyon. Starting at the canyon's dramatic rim, the trail meanders and winds gently away from it, where the dense forest enchants differently

Fall colors along Transept Trail.

at each hour of the day as the sun's rays light up the space according to its celestial trajectory. Mixed pine, quaking aspen, and oak trees decorate the landscape, making for interesting habitat for Kaibab squirrels and cliff chipmunks. This is a pleasant early-morning or sunset hike.

3 Bridle Path

DISTANCE: 1.9 miles (3.1 km) one-way; allow 1 hour.
DIFFICULTY: Easy; hard-packed dirt and gravel.
WATER: None.
OTHER: Pets on a 6-foot leash and bicycles are permitted.

This path parallels the road that connects Grand Canyon Lodge with the North Kaibab Trailhead. Parking is available at the North Kaibab Trailhead, but it can fill up quickly. As a hike in and of itself, it cannot compare to the grand views of the other trails, although it does extend through the forest. Its purpose is as a connector path for hikers staying at the lodge who would rather walk to the North Kaibab Trailhead than drive and park.

4 Widforss Trail

DISTANCE: 9.6 miles (15.5 km) round trip; allow 6 hours.
DIFFICULTY: Moderate; several steep up-and-downs on dirt and gravel.
WATER: None.
OTHER: Toilets at trailhead.

Take the dirt road (Point Sublime Road) 0.25 mile (0.4 km) south of the road to Cape Royal for 1 mile (1.6 km); the Widforss Trail parking area is on the left.

The Widforss Trailhead is a quarter-mile from Highway 67 on Point Sublime Road, at the edge of Harvey Meadow. Leaving the meadow, the trail contours along the rim on a ridge of Kaibab Limestone deposited 270 to 250 million years ago. This ancient bedrock is rich with fossils of sea creatures that long ago inhabited the vanished seabed.

Trail namesake Gunnar Widforss sketching on the North Rim, ca. 1934.

Views along Widforss Trail.

Halfway to Widforss Point, the trail leads away from the rim and into a forest thick with ponderosa pine, quaking aspen, white fir, and blue spruce. Eventually emerging once again at the rim, the trail culminates at Widforss Point, revealing a stunning view across the canyon toward the South Rim. On a clear day, Flagstaff's San Francisco Peaks (elevation 12,633 feet/3,850 m), Arizona's highest mountain range, can be seen in the distance.

The trail parallels The Transept, a long tributary canyon to the even longer Bright Angel Canyon. Notice how North Rim tributary canyons tend to be much longer than those on the South Rim. This is due to the sedimentary rocks that make up the Grand Canyon dipping slightly to the south. Precipitation on the North Rim runs into the Grand Canyon, whereas precipitation on the South Rim flows away from the canyon. Thus, the cutting of side canyons is greater on the north.

Hiking on the Widforss Trail.

⑤ Uncle Jim Trail

DISTANCE: 5 miles (8 km) round trip; allow 3 hours.
DIFFICULTY: Moderate; well-marked, with gentle gradients on dirt and gravel.
WATER: None.
OTHER: Mules also use this trail; when they are encountered, step off the trail, stay still, and follow the wrangler's instructions.

Starting at the North Kaibab Trail parking lot as part of the Ken Patrick Trail, after 0.9 mile (1.5 km), the Uncle Jim Trail splits off to the right and makes a loop that leads to an overlook of the North Kaibab Trail.

Named for game warden James T. Owen, the Uncle Jim Trail rambles through the forest over an undulating surface pockmarked with sinkholes. This

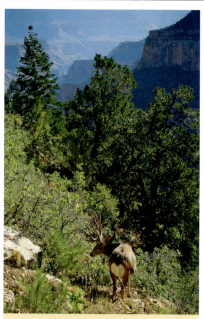

Mule deer browsing along the edge of North Rim.

topography is known as "karst," a term derived from similar geologic features in the Karst district of the Adriatic coast. Water seeping down through the Kaibab Limestone dissolves the rock and creates caves whose roofs occasionally collapse, forming these circular sinkholes. Sinkholes that hold rainwater become important water sources for wildlife. The retention of moisture may also encourage the growth of certain plants. Here on the Kaibab Plateau, this sometimes facilitates the flourishing of aspen, while ponderosa pine are restricted to slightly drier zones.

Uncle Jim Owen, right, leading a hunting party, August 1913.

⑥ Ken Patrick Trail

DISTANCE: 9.8 miles (15.8 km) one way; allow 6 hours.
DIFFICULTY: Moderate; several steep up-and-downs on dirt and gravel; some obscure sections.
WATER: None.
OTHER: Requires a shuttle if hiking the entire distance.

This trail can be accessed from either the North Kaibab Trail parking lot or Point Imperial parking lot. Some sections are rocky and make sudden descents and ascents. The Outlet and Fuller Fires have affected the integrity of the trail, which in places may be vague and/or confused by old fire roads. Also, "blow-down"—fallen timber—can make for challenging walking.

However, hikers are rewarded with many fine views into the canyon as well as of Mount Hayden, Nankoweap Basin, Painted Desert, and—on a clear day—Navajo Mountain on the far horizon. The trail is named for Ken Patrick, a park ranger who died in the line of duty.

Branching off the Ken Patrick Trail is the Old Bright Angel Creek Trail (AKA Old Kaibab Trail), which, after 7.8 miles (12.6 km), intersects with the North Kaibab near Roaring Springs. This old, steep, overgrown, and unmaintained trail is of historic interest only.

View from Ken Patrick Trail.

7 Arizona Trail
(Arizona National Scenic Trail)

DISTANCE: 12.1 miles (19.5 km) one-way; allow 7 hours.
DIFFICULTY: Moderate.
WATER: None.
OTHER: Pets on a 6-foot leash and bicycles are permitted.

The 800-mile-long Arizona Trail was the dream of Dale Shewalter, who envisioned a cross-state trail in the 1970s. In 1985, while working as a Flagstaff schoolteacher, he walked from Nogales to the Utah state line to explore the feasibility of a trail traversing Arizona. *For more information, go to aztrail.org.*

This section of the Arizona Trail enters the park about two miles east of the North Rim Entrance Station. It roughly parallels Arizona Highway 67 and passes through Harvey Meadow near the Widforss Trailhead before connecting with the North Kaibab Trail. About .5 mile (.8 km) after the Arizona Trail enters the park, a short, signed trail leads to an abandoned historic fire lookout tower. During the 1970s, environmental writer Edward Abbey, of *Desert Solitaire* and *The Monkey Wrench Gang* fame, manned this fire tower located east of the main entrance station.

8 North Kaibab Trail

DISTANCE: 14 miles (22.5 km) one-way to the Bright Angel Campground and Colorado River. Permit is required for overnight use.
DIFFICULTY: Difficult, but maintained.
WATER: Supai Tunnel (intermittent), Manzanita Rest Area (intermittent); check with Backcountry Information Center for status before hiking.

The North Kaibab Trail is the only regularly maintained trail leading from the North Rim to the Colorado River. However, this is no casual stroll. It stretches 14 miles (22.5 km) one-way to the Colorado River via Roaring Springs Canyon to its junction with Bright Angel Canyon.

Shorter day hikes can be taken to Supai Tunnel (4 miles/6.4 km round trip) and Manzanita Rest Area (a strenuous 10.8 miles/17.4 km round trip). Carry plenty of drinking water, as water is not guaranteed at any of the designated water stops. And remember that it's a long and uphill climb back to the rim.

The trail begins in a cloud of ponderosa pine, maple, fir, and aspen, with a healthy undergrowth of bracken fern. The steep descent through the Coconino Sandstone layer leads to the first available water station at Supai Tunnel (1.7 miles/2.7 km), although water is not guaranteed (check with NPS rangers before you go). At 5.5 miles (8.9 km), Manzanita Rest Area offers cool shade, restrooms, and a water station, although,

again, water is not guaranteed.

At 8.4 miles (13.5 km), just off the main trail, is a worthwhile destination: Ribbon Falls. From here the trail descends into the more desert-like ecosystem of the canyon floor, following Bright Angel Creek and eventually passing through Cottonwood Campground. Before reaching Bright Angel Campground, the trail enters the Inner Gorge, where the canyon walls are closer together, giving the hiker a feeling of being somewhat boxed in. The Inner Gorge is also where a series of bridges leads from one side of the creek to another and back again.

Mules also use this trail; when mules approach, step off the trail, remain quiet, and follow the wrangler's instructions.

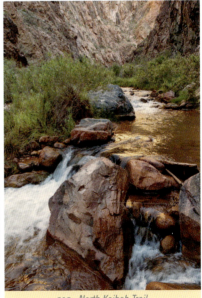

TOP: *North Kaibab Trail*
ABOVE: *Bright Angel Creek*

Point Sublime Road & Viewpoint

▲▲ **DISTANCE:** 17.7 miles (28.5 km) one-way; allow at least 2 hours each way.
▲ **DIFFICULTY:** High-clearance and four-wheel drive vehicle strongly recommended.
▲ **WATER:** None.
▲ **OTHER:** Popular with mountain bikers.

The westernmost viewpoint in the park, Point Sublime is reached by continuing on the road past the Widforss Trailhead. At the very least, a high-clearance vehicle, and possibly a four-wheel-drive vehicle, is necessary. Camping is allowed with a backcountry camping permit. Inquire about road conditions and possible closures at the Backcountry Office before heading out. (Take this warning seriously. The cost for a tow truck to Point Sublime is more than $1,000.) Along this road are some huge ponderosa pines; one may be the state's largest. It has a circumference of 204 inches (518 cm) at chest height.

In 1880, using the Powell Survey's recently completed map, geologist Clarence Dutton made an overland trip to the Toroweap Overlook and gazed down on the basaltic rocks tumbling into the canyon. He then traveled into the Tapeats Amphitheater, down to the Esplanade, across Surprise Valley to Deer Creek, and finally descended to the river. Once back on the rim, he continued up onto the Kaibab Plateau and into the thick forest. Heading south, he broke out of the trees to see another part of the Grand Canyon.

As he described the experience in the U.S. Geological Survey's 1882 annual report, "The earth suddenly sinks at our feet to illimitable depths. In an instant, in the twinkling of an eye, the awful scene is before us. Reaching the extreme verge the packs are cast off, and sitting up on the edge we contemplate the most sublime and awe-inspiring spectacle in the world. We name it Point Sublime."

Deer Creek

Point Imperial
🏕️🚻
8803ft
2683m

2.6mi
4.2km

Cape Royal Road

3.0mi
4.9km

6 Ken Patrick Trail

THE Y

3.1mi
5.0km

Greenland Lake

🏕️ 8480ft
2585m
Vista Encantada

POINT IMPERIAL DETAIL

Point Imperial
🏕️🚻
8803ft
2683m

Paved road	🚻	Restrooms
Unpaved road	🏕️	Picnic area
4-wheel drive road		
Trail		

🏕️ 8480ft
2585m
Vista Encantada

14.5mi
23.3km

Roosevelt Point Trail
9
Roosevelt Point
8470ft
2582m

GRAND CANYON

*WALHALLA
PLATEAU*

WALHALLA GLADES

NATCHI
CANYON

• Francois Matthes
Point
8020ft
2445m

Cape Final Trail
10
2.1mi
3.4km

Cape Fin
7916
2413

• Honan Point
7922ft
2415m

Walhalla Glades Pueblo

Walhalla Overlook
7998ft
2438m

*Cliff
Spring*

• Thor Temple
6741ft
2055m

Cliff Spring Trail **11**

Angels Window

Cape Royal
7865ft
2397m

12 Cape Royal Trail

• Wotans Throne
7721ft
2353m

Northeast Area

CAPE ROYAL ROAD

The turn onto the Cape Royal Road is about 10 miles (16 km) south of the entrance station, or 3 miles (4.8 km) north of the visitor center. In 5.4 miles (8.7 km), there is a fork. Left leads to Point Imperial at 2.6 miles (4.2 km); right continues 14.5 miles (23.3 km) to Cape Royal. Although the distances are modest, it can take a whole morning, afternoon, or more to stop, walk/hike, and enjoy the many viewpoints along the way.

Point Imperial

Point Imperial viewpoint is a 20-minute, 11-mile (18-km) drive from the visitor center. After making a left at the Y on Cape Royal Road, the ravages of the Fuller Fire will be apparent. In June 2016, lightning started a fire that the forest service and park service hoped to manage as a low-intensity blaze. But instead of summer rains damping the fire, dry, windy weather moved in, fanning the flames. Eventually, the Fuller Fire burned 14,500 acres (5,868 hectares). The thick stands of aspen that grew after the Outlet Fire (2000) are mostly burnt sticks,

but at their bases, new growth is already occurring.

The highest viewpoint along the North Rim, Point Imperial—8,803 feet (2,683 m)—provides a stunning panoramic vista that stretches from the Vermilion Cliffs to the Echo Cliffs and far into the Painted Desert. The dome-shaped mountain beyond the Echo Cliffs is Navajo Mountain, some 80 miles (129 km) away,

Point Imperial, at 8,803 feet (2,683 m), one of the North Rim's highest viewpoints.

straddling the Utah-Arizona border. On an exceptionally clear day, the Henry Mountains, 133 miles (214 km) away in southern Utah, can be seen.

In the foreground is the Coconino Sandstone monolith Mount Hayden, named after Charles Trumbull Hayden, who arrived in Arizona on the first Butterfield Overland stage in 1857 and eventually established Hayden's Ferry on the Salt River, the site of modern-day Tempe, Arizona.

To the left, the large notch in the near ridge marks the appropriately named Saddle Mountain. Also visible from here is the spot at which the Colorado River emerges from the relatively narrow gorge of Marble Canyon into the broad eastern Grand Canyon. The river, which is out of view, lies beneath the distant eastern rim.

Back at the Y, continue straight to reach Cape Royal. In about 1 mile (1.6 km) at a sharp right bend in the road, a painted crosswalk, an inconspicuous sign, and tiny pullout mark the crossing of the Ken Patrick Trail. Another 1.5 miles (2.4 km) is the small turnout for Greenland Lake.

GREENLAND LAKE

Rain and snowmelt seeping through the porous Kaibab Limestone can dissolve underlying stone to create sinkholes.

Greenland Lake, the sinkhole that became a wildlife-attracting pond.

Some, such as Greenland Lake, accumulate enough silt and clay to make them relatively impervious to water, thus creating small, wildlife-attracting ponds. This fairly reliable water source was used as a waterhole by the cattle that once grazed the plateau. (In the 1890s, Bar Z cattlemen erected the small cabin here to store salt and other supplies.)

Walk around to the far side of the pond, watching out for the thorny New Mexican locust. The edge of the pond is fringed with sedges and tiny rushes, grasslike plants that favor wet ground. Little pocket-gopher eskers (mounds of freshly tilled soil) mark the lake's banks, but it's unlikely that you'll actually see the stealthy mammal.

Look for the harmless wandering

garter snakes (*Thamnophis elegans vagrans*) that often lurk here. If you are very lucky, you may see one dining on a salamander, an earthworm, or a Great Basin spadefoot toad (*Scaphiopus intermontanus*).

Vista Encantada

The name Vista Encantada was changed to Vista Encantadora (*enchanting* instead of *enchanted*) in 1941 by Harold C. Bryant, then superintendent of the park. Later, it was changed back. Regardless of whether it is enchanting or enchanted, the vista is definitely lovely.

Beyond the far eastern rim lies Navajo and Hopi country. Much of the land in the distance is the Painted Desert, so-called because of its myriad layers of colorful claystones, sandstones, and other sedimentary deposits. Most of those sedimentary layers were laid down during the Mesozoic Era, the Age of Reptiles, when Arizona sat closer to the equator and the climate was hot and tropical. Being Mesozoic makes them younger than any of the major rock layers in the Grand Canyon.

Roosevelt Point

On his first visit to the Grand Canyon in May 1903, Theodore Roosevelt instructed, "Leave it as it is. You cannot improve upon it. The ages have been at work on it, and man can only mar it." Surprisingly, the man arguably most influential in helping preserve the Grand Canyon

didn't get a single feature named after him until July 1996, when this viewpoint was dedicated by then-Secretary of the Interior Bruce Babbitt.

9 Roosevelt Point Trail

DISTANCE: 0.2 mile (0.3 km) round trip; allow 20 minutes.
DIFFICULTY: Easy.
WATER: None.

The trail begins at the Roosevelt Point parking area and loops through secluded woodland, offering spectacular canyon views and benches for relaxing.

Preservation Timeline

1893: President Benjamin Harrison sets aside much of the "Grand Cañon of the Colorado" as Grand Canyon Forest Reserve, but allows grazing, mining, and lumbering to continue.
1906: President Theodore Roosevelt declares portions of the reserve to be a federal game preserve.
1908: President Theodore Roosevelt establishes Grand Canyon National Monument by presidential proclamation.
1919: Congress changes the monument's status to national park.
1979: The United Nations Environmental, Scientific and Cultural Organization (UNESCO) recognizes Grand Canyon as a World Heritage Site.

🔟 Cape Final Trail

DISTANCE: 4.2 miles (6.8 km) round trip; allow 2 to 3 hours.
DIFFICULTY: Moderate; several up-and-downs on dirt and gravel.
WATER: None.

The trailhead parking lot is 2.4 miles (3.9 km) north of the Cape Royal parking lot. Geologist Clarence Dutton named this point in 1880, writing "Point Final is doubtless the most interesting spot on the Kaibab. In pure grandeur, it is about the same as Point Sublime [but] the two differ much in the characteristics of the scenery."

Below this eastern edge of the Walhalla Plateau, the Grand Canyon Supergroup is magnificently exposed. These Precambrian sedimentary and volcanic rocks are the remnants of ancient mountains.

Walhalla Overlook & Walhalla Glades Pueblo

Below, the long drainage of Unkar Creek meanders toward the Colorado River. The river sweeps around the edge of Unkar Delta, the site of one of the largest known prehistoric settlements within Grand Canyon.

In the distance are the Echo Cliffs and Painted Desert country. The Navajo Reservation occupies much of that land, with the exception of the Hopi Reservation, which is sited roughly in the middle of Navajo country.

The mouth of the Little Colorado River Gorge, a spectacular canyon in its own right, appears to the southeast, entrenched in the Painted Desert. Up the gorge is the sacred Hopi *sipapuni*, a strange travertine spring that bubbles with carbon dioxide gas and protects the entrance to the Hopi Underworld. Near the river's mouth, several small caves drip with salt stalactites; a magical place,

Cape Final

Ancestral Puebloan pottery from an excavation on the Walhalla Plateau.

⑪ Cliff Spring Trail

DISTANCE: 0.8 mile (1.3 km) round trip; allow 1 hour.
DIFFICULTY: Easy, but with a few steep steps.
WATER: None; do not drink from the spring.
OTHER: There is a small prehistoric granary along the trail. Please do not enter it or touch the walls.

it is where Hopis ceremonially collect salt and leave behind tiny fetishes to become encrusted by the briny solution.

Behind and across the road is a short path leading to the Walhalla Glades Pueblo. This pueblo, excavated by Douglas Schwartz and his crew, consisted of at least nine rooms and was occupied between AD 1100 and 1150. Though this one small site doesn't suggest it, a thousand years ago, the Walhalla Plateau was heavily occupied on a seasonal basis. The majority of sites here are located along the edge of ridges that overlook drainages. Travel between the rim and the river, albeit strenuous, would have been a common occurrence.

The trail to Cliff Spring begins directly across from a small pullout located on a curve (watch for traffic) 0.3 mile (0.5 km) down the road from Cape Royal. The trail descends a forested ravine and ends at a chest-high boulder under a large overhang. The tiny spring on the cliff side of the boulder may not be flowing, and in any event, drinking its water is not recommended. It is, however, often one of the better places to observe birds as they come in for a drink or to hunt for food.

In 1913, Teddy Roosevelt and his hunting party camped along the Cliff Spring Trail. Teddy's cousin, Nicholas Roosevelt, described the idyllic spot: "[T]urning a corner came in sight of an open gallery in the rocks…over which a ledge projected, making it a perfect shelter from all storms. …[N]ear the end of it was a beautiful, clear spring, known as Cliff Spring, by which grew some enormous pine trees. …We made camp in what would have made an ideal robbers' den in the Middle Ages."

Cape Royal

Cape Royal was named by geologist and US Army officer Clarence Dutton in 1882, who called it a "congregation of wonderful structures, countless and vast, profound lateral chasms."

12 Cape Royal Trail

DISTANCE: 0.8 mile (1.3 km) round trip; allow 1 hour.
DIFFICULTY: Easy; flat paved trail.
WATER: None.
OTHER: About 23 miles (37 km) from the visitor center, or a roughly 45-minute drive one-way.

Starting at the southeast side of the Cape Royal parking area, this trail offers an easy walk, with views of the canyon, Angels Window (a natural arch created by erosion), and the Colorado River. The short walk out to Cape Royal passes plants typical of the piñon-juniper woodland (a habitat typically found at lower elevations), including cliffrose, Utah juniper, sage, piñon, wild currant, buffalo berry, Utah serviceberry, and fernbush. Warm, dry updrafts from the inner canyon seem to make this point of land inhospitable for the conifers (ponderosa pine, spruce, and fir) found elsewhere at this elevation (nearly 8,000 feet/2,438 m).

Continue out to Cape Royal, of which Theodore Roosevelt wrote, "From the southernmost point of this tableland the view of the Canyon left the beholder solemn with the sense of awe. ...The dawn and the evening twilight were brooding mysteries over the dusk of the abyss; night shrouded its immensity, but did not hide it."

As you walk this trail, note the neat rows of small holes pecked into the trunks of piñons and junipers by red-

Little Colorado River Gorge   Marble Platform/Navajo Nation   Nankoweap Mesa   Nankoweap Creek

Cape Royal

naped sapsuckers. Dark-eyed juncos, scrub jays, mountain chickadees, or white-breasted or pygmy nuthatches also may be seen or heard. Uinta chipmunks

and variegated rock squirrels often come begging, but don't feed them, or any other wildlife.

Confluence of the Colorado River and Little Colorado River

Kwagunt Butte   Chuar Butte   Mt. Hayden

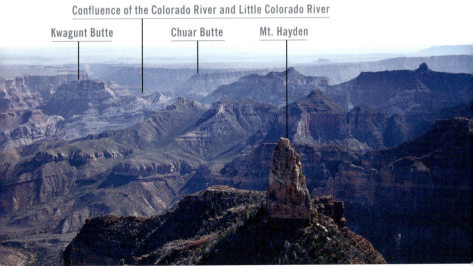

San Francisco Peaks

Coronado Butte

Vishnu Temple

Angels Window

Kaibab Limestone (and most other Grand Canyon formations) is fractured by many vertical cracks, called joints. Joints may form when rocks are stressed, such as during uplift (Kaibab Limestone was formed millions of years ago in a warm, shallow sea and is now more than 7,000 feet/2,134 m above sea level), or when the weight of overlying formations is removed. The Kaibab is Permian in age, and it's presumed that thousands of feet of younger layers once covered the region. Joints are further widened by the forces of erosion, such as freeze/thaw action. As two parallel joints erode, a relatively thin wall between the joints may be created. This wall weathers thinner and thinner, until one day, a hole is worn through and a window is born.

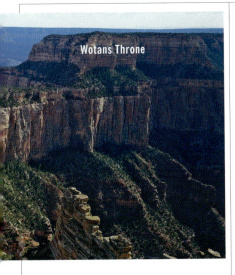

Wotans Throne

North Bass Trail, built by prospector and entrepreneur William Bass, was never a well-constructed or regularly maintained route. The National Park Service and volunteers from the American Conservation Experience have been working to restore it, but it is still considered primitive.

Northwest of Powell Plateau are the verdant Deer and Tapeats Creeks. From the rim, these canyon jewels are accessed by the primitive Thunder River Trail (or by the shorter Bill Hall Trail that drops off Monument Point). Thunder River lives up to its name, gushing out of a cave in the Muav Limestone and cascading down to Tapeats Creek; this is possibly the only place in the world where a river flows into a creek.

For current information and permits to hike these trails, contact the NPS Backcountry Information Center.

Less-established North Rim Hikes

A few more North Rim trails—North Bass and Thunder River among them—can be found on maps, but most are not maintained, are difficult to access, and require backcountry hiking skills, especially orienteering.

Thunder River

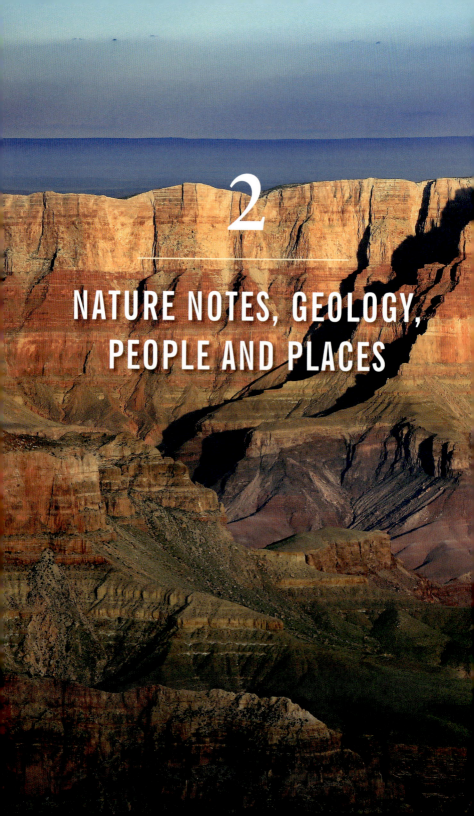

2

NATURE NOTES, GEOLOGY, PEOPLE AND PLACES

Nature Notes

HISTORY ON BARK

While hiking through a gorgeous North Rim aspen grove, you may notice names, words, dates, pictures, and brands carved into the trees' white-barked trunks. These are called dendroglyphs, and archaeologists and historians have recorded nearly two hundred of them on the North Rim. Although scattered throughout stands of aspen, most are located along old roads or near water. They date from the 1890s to the 1950s. Many of the earliest ones were made primarily by cowboys tending cattle during the short summer months. However, in the area near Point Imperial, the dendroglyphs mostly date to December and January.

Merle "Cowhide" Adams, a longtime Kaibab Plateau cowboy, cleared up the mystery. He recalled that after the autumn roundup, during which cattle were moved off the high plateau to the lower House Rock Valley, cowboys would return to "ride the points"—all points of the compass—searching for strays after the first snowfall forced them to the canyon rim. While these old carvings help piece together the history of the North Rim, it is considered very poor form (not to mention illegal) to carve new ones.

Dendroglyphs on aspen trees reveal historic timelines.

WITCH'S BROOM

Dwarf mistletoe, a relative of true mistletoes, or Christmas mistletoe, parasitize conifers instead of hardwoods. It's not uncommon to see yellow-orange shoots growing from infected stems of a ponderosa pine. An older infection is readily recognized by the way the pine's branches become very dense and misshapen, forming a "witch's broom." Dwarf mistletoe spreads when its berries explosively discharge the seed. Flying up to an astounding 60 miles per hour and as far as 40 feet, the sticky seed may land on another pine branch and take root. Wildfires are one of the primary natural controls limiting the spread of this parasite.

THE KAIBAB MULE DEER MYTH

The large-eared mule deer—flatlanders, compared to bighorn sheep—have always been more common on the North Rim; there is simply more deer habitat here. However, that didn't faze various early wildlife managers. Between 1927 and 1931, about sixty fawns were transported from the North Rim to the South. Superintendent Minor Tillotson wrote that the "friendly little creatures" were a great tourist favorite. By 1934, Tillotson's friendly little creatures had so increased in number that they were over-browsing the Grand Canyon Village area. But this was a minor problem in comparison to what had happened on the Kaibab Plateau a couple of decades earlier.

After hunting mountain lions on the North Rim in 1913 with game warden Jimmy Owens, Theodore Roosevelt

Adaptable mule deer are found from rim to river in all park habitats.

remarked, "One important feature of his work is to keep down the larger beasts and birds of prey, the archenemies of the deer, mountain sheep, and grouse; and the most formidable among these foes of the harmless wildlife are the cougars." A prevailing attitude of the time, this ultimately tipped nature's balance between predators and prey on the Kaibab Plateau.

Within a few years of ceaseless shooting, trapping, and poisoning of coyotes, mountain lions, and Mexican gray wolves on the North Rim, hunters, forest managers, and visitors began to report that the Kaibab deer herd was exploding in numbers.

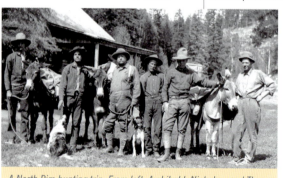

A North Rim hunting trip. From left: Archibald, Nicholas, and Theodore Roosevelt; Jim Owens; Quentin Roosevelt; Jesse Cummins.

A browse line—the boundary between normal growth and stripped, eaten-back growth that was as high as deer could reach—became evident in the forest, and forage was deteriorating.

Nature soon delivered her own brand of management. During the winter of 1924–1925, thousands of deer starved to death; the population decline continued for a decade. From this disaster, wildlife managers came to view the Kaibab deer herd as the archetype of ungulate irruption (population explosion) brought on by excessive predator control.

In recent years, biologists have re-examined the Kaibab incident in light of new research regarding predator/prey relationships. Their findings indicate that earlier population figures are open to question, the increase in deer populations may not have been as dramatic as previously presented, and the lack of predators may have played only a small role in the drama. All that can be said for sure is that there was an apparent increase in the number of deer between 1914 and 1924, and that range forage deteriorated.

By the late 1880s, perhaps 20,000 cattle, 200,000 sheep, and unknown numbers of horses and dairy cows were grazing on the Kaibab Plateau. By 1906, through government regulation and declining forage, livestock numbers had been significantly reduced. Did reduced livestock grazing allow vegetation to rebound, triggering an increase in the deer population?

Biologists believe that food supply is a major factor in determining prey populations. In turn, prey numbers influence predator populations. This is opposite of the conventional wisdom of earlier wildlife managers. Predators play a minor role in controlling prey densities. Studies done on the Kaibab indicate that lion predation, even at the highest rates measured, does not prevent the deer from increasing, provided that there is adequate browse. Whatever the real dynamics of the deer population might have been, the Kaibab deer story is an excellent example of how science, conservation, politics, and management interact.

Wouldn't Owens, Roosevelt, and other early sportsmen be surprised to know that the mountain lion, "destroyer of the deer...lord of stealthy murder... with a heart both craven and cruel," is now viewed as a necessary spoke on the wheel of life? It is hoped that as our ecological knowledge expands, so will our wisdom to become better stewards.

MOUNTAIN LIONS

Studying the secretive mountain lion has always been problematic for biologists. At Grand Canyon, they are gaining insights through the study of DNA samples from field-collected hair, tissue, and scat (feces). DNA allows the scientists to identify individual lions, establish kinship, and determine minimum population estimates. To aid in the collection of DNA samples, scientists have placed scented posts at various locations. The lions rub against the post, leaving hair behind. A few lions have also been radio-tagged to record their movements.

Radio-tagged lions were tracked for

Mountain lions are the the park's largest obligate carnivores.

nearly a year to determine home-range size and location in the park. These ranges varied from 76 to 185 square miles. Although most lions remain on the rims (where there is more food), one lion made an astounding journey down from the South Rim, across the Colorado River, and up to the North Rim in eight hours.

BISON

An increasingly common sight in the meadows of the North Rim and Kaibab Plateau are herds of American bison (popularly called buffalo). The bison arrived in Arizona through the efforts of Charles Jesse "Buffalo" Jones, an ex-buffalo hunter. By the end of nineteenth century, the bison were nearing extinction, and Jones became concerned. In earlier days, he had taken advantage of the booming market for bison hides and meat, but, angered by the merciless waste, he eventually put away his rifle. Instead, Jones turned to roping bison and breeding them in hopes of perpetuating the species.

He also dreamed of crossing bison bulls with black Scottish Galloway cows to produce a hybrid animal that would have the virtues of each parent: silky hair; rich, tender meat; immunity to disease; harsh weather survivability; and the capacity to eat meager, scrubby browse.

Through his friendship with President Theodore Roosevelt, Jones received a federal permit in January 1906 to fence a large area on the North Rim near Bright Angel Point for bison and other big game animals. Later that same year, President Roosevelt established the Grand Canyon Game Preserve, which included the entire Kaibab Plateau.

Additionally, the Secretary of Agriculture wrote a letter to the Secretary of the Interior, allowing Jones to obtain a loan of bison from Yellowstone "for the purpose of experimenting in the hybridizing of buffalo and cattle, the Government to retain a certain percentage of the produce."

By issuing stock certificates, Jones was able to raise money to purchase Scottish Galloway cows and additional bison from Texas, New Mexico, Kansas, Nebraska, and Manitoba. However, getting the animals to the Kaibab was no small feat. Most arrived via train at Lund, Utah, the closest railhead, then were herded across more than 150 miles of inhospitable desert to the cool forests of the Kaibab. The bison refused to walk during the heat of the day, so the wranglers coaxed them along at night with a wagon full of wheat.

When the bison didn't seem to thrive

Bison have adapted to the diverse habitats of the rim and outlying areas.

on the Kaibab, they were moved to the grasslands of House Rock Valley. Producing hybrids, or "cattalos," as Jones called them, proved to be challenging. Bison and Galloways bred reluctantly, and male calves from the first cross-breeding were either aborted or caused the death of the cow. Heifer calves survived, but when bred to bison bulls, produced sterile male calves; the thick coats of the latter kept their reproductive organs at too high a temperature. Only by breeding back to domestic cattle could fertile males be obtained.

Unfortunately for Jones, the experimenting took too long, and investors attempted to recoup their losses by claiming the domestic animals. One old cattalo, with a definite bison body shape but covered with blotches of white fur, was put on display at Jacob Lake, where tourists paid fifty cents to see it. By 1909, in large part due to the failed forced cross-breeding effort, the bison herd was reduced to around twenty animals. Despite the near-total failure, this small group of bison survived and perpetuated themselves with little to no man-

agement until 1927, when ninety-eight free-ranging descendants were sold to the state of Arizona. (Genetic testing has confirmed that modern-day offspring still carry domestic cattle genes.)

Originally, the Arizona Game and Fish Department intended to manage the herd at about 100 animals. Hunts now held once a year on a lottery basis are considered among the toughest in the state because of the difficulty in locating the animals. Hunters are more likely to see pronghorn and jackrabbits.

Though the bison (or cattalo) were supposed to be contained within their House Rock Valley game range, which covers about 60,000 acres of sagebrush and grassland, over the years, they have wandered back into the adjacent Kaibab National Forest and Grand Canyon National Park, much to the chagrin of park rangers. Presumably, as bison hunting increased, the animals learned that being in the park was a safe refuge.

The animals do considerable damage to vegetation, compact the soil (a bull may weigh more than a ton), and pollute water sources. Herd numbers have exploded to more than 600, and biologists estimate the herd could top 1,500 within ten years. Bison can live up to thirty years and cows can bear calves for twenty years. They eat upwards of thirty-five pounds of vegetation daily, another thing that causes the park service and wildlife managers some concern.

Elk are more likely to be seen outside of the park.

Although this particular bison herd was introduced, some biologists now feel that the Kaibab Plateau area falls under the historic range for bison and, therefore, should be managed as native wildlife. A plan to reduce herd numbers through round-ups and special hunts to mitigate the animals' impact on other native plant and animal species has been proposed.

While they may appear to be slow-moving animals, they can easily outrun a person. Never approach them on foot.

WAPITI, OR AMERICAN ELK

Although rarely occurring on the Arizona Strip, elk are truly majestic animals and a delight to see, especially in the autumn, when 1,000-pound bulls sport a huge rack on their head. Many biologists prefer to call them wapiti, the Shawnee Indian word for "white rump," to avoid confusion with the European elk, which refers to moose. In the early 1900s, E. D. Woolley, along with Senator Reed Smoot, tried to have elk introduced to the Grand Canyon Game Preserve on the Kaibab Plateau, ultimately to no avail.

There have been some reports of year-ling male elk seen in House Rock Valley; these are probably animals that have migrated south from Utah. You are more likely to encounter them in the meadows and foothills of the Kaibab Plateau, where fires often produce high-quality elk habitat. Elk are predominately grazers, relying on the grasses, deciduous shrubs, and herbaceous plants that tend to sprout after a fire.

DESERT BIGHORN SHEEP

The magnificent desert bighorn sheep once roamed most of the American Southwest, but over-hunting and the introduction of large numbers of domestic sheep (which carried diseases fatal to wild sheep) caused a catastrophic decline in bighorn numbers by the early twentieth century. Fortunately, the Grand Canyon is a sanctuary for this species, and they are occasionally seen in Bright Angel Canyon, around Cliff Spring, and in Kanab Canyon. Since the sheep are unmolested here, they are usually not bothered by human presence.

Bighorns live in a vertical world. While deer organize their mating society by

Desert bighorn sheep are the park's largest native animal.

evicting other bucks and claiming all the does in a certain territory, the harem strategy doesn't work for bighorns. The ewes are not very herdable—they are more like popcorn, hopping and jumping from one tiny ledge to even tinier nubbins. The dominant ram must guard each ewe one at a time and mate with her before moving to the next receptive female.

KAIBAB SQUIRRELS

A treat on the North Rim is catching a glimpse of a Kaibab squirrel, a unique form of the tassel-eared group of tree squirrels. The Kaibab squirrel has a dark charcoal head and body, a rust patch on its back, and a striking, snow-white, fluffy tail. This squirrel is native only to the Kaibab Plateau. Like the South Rim's Abert squirrel, it occurs only where there

is ponderosa pine, and depends almost exclusively on that particular pine for food and nesting materials.

The Kaibab squirrel, one of the rarest mammals in the national park system.

The isolated population of uniquely colored Kaibab squirrels is an excellent example of what biologists call "insular evolution." Islands, whether they are in the middle of the sea or a biologically isolated land habitat, often have species that are endemic (restricted) to them.

In this case, the "island" is the ponderosa pine forest of the Kaibab Plateau, surrounded by desert.

How did the squirrels reach the plateau? One scenario suggests that before the Grand Canyon existed, ancestors of these squirrels lived in one huge, intact pine forest. As the Colorado River carved the canyon, the forest became fragmented and the resident squirrel populations became separated from one another. Over eons, the isolated North Rim population began to exhibit the genes for dark body fur and white tails.

The problem with this theory is one of timing. Ponderosa pine did not spread into northern Arizona (presumably from the south) until a mere 10,000 to 11,000 years ago, during the waning days of the last ice age. The Grand Canyon is at least several million years old. So how did the pine make its way across the canyon, and how and when did the squirrel follow? So far, these are unsolved mysteries.

One thing known for certain is the important role these squirrels play in the health of ponderosa pine forests. Interwoven around the roots of the pines are specialized fungi called "microrhiza," which absorb water and minerals from the soil and produce growth stimulants that are absorbed by the tree. The pine photosynthesizes sugars for itself and the fungi, a beautiful symbiotic relationship. The fungi grow underground fruiting bodies called false truffles. But how do the spores within the truffles get spread around to new pine seedlings? That's where the squirrels enter the story. They sniff out the false truffles (even under a foot of snow), dig them up, and eat with relish. Then, as the squirrels defecate on the run, they spread fungal spores through the forest.

CHIPMUNKS AND GROUND SQUIRRELS

Besides mule deer, probably the most frequently encountered mammal will be one of several types of ground squirrels. During some summers, the squirrels may be quite common and can become pests, especially if people feed them. (Reminder: Feeding wildlife is not only illegal, but—given the risk of being bitten—a very bad idea.)

Ground squirrels are large, with long, bushy tails like tree squirrels.

Of the several species of chipmunks on the North Rim, the cliff chipmunk lives up to its name by residing primarily along the rocky rim edges. The Uinta chipmunk and golden-mantled ground squirrel tend to be found in the pine forest, and the least chipmunk is primarily a dweller of grassy areas within the forest. The slightly larger and more robust golden-mantled ground squirrel looks like a large chipmunk but lacks stripes on its head. Occasionally, the even larger variegated rock squirrel may be seen scampering along the rocky cliffs or trying to get into an unattended backpack.

POCKET GOPHERS

Pocket gophers spend most of their life underground, digging elaborate tunnels (feeding burrows) to the base of plants so they can eat the roots; sometimes, they will also pull down the leafy part of the plant for a meal. They have sturdy incisor teeth and long claws on their front feet, fur-lined cheek pouches, small eyes, and a nearly naked but highly sensitive tail. The tail acts as a "feeler," allowing the pocket gopher to run rapidly backward in the burrow.

Where a burrow nears the surface, a mound of dirt is thrown up. Usually, the gopher plugs its burrow opening to keep out predators like weasels and snakes. When the ground is covered by snow, gophers tunnel through the snow along the snow/ground interface to forage. Soil is pushed into these snow tunnels, and when the snow melts, a network of earthen cores remains on the surface.

RAPTOR MIGRATION

In 1987, field biologist Chuck LaRue noted that the fall migration of hawks and other raptors along the intermountain migratory flyway from Alaska to Mexico streamed right over the Grand Canyon region. From 1991 until 2011, observers for HawkWatch International conducted surveys of migrating raptors over the Grand Canyon. At the top of

the food pyramid, large raptor populations indicate healthy prey populations and (presumably) productive habitats. Migration counts are an efficient and economical method for monitoring the regional status of raptors, which serve as important indicators of ecosystem well-being.

Red-tailed hawk

During migration, raptors rely on thermal uplifts and ridge-line updrafts to conserve energy. Their migration over the Grand Canyon is unique in that it is not guided by mountain ridges but rather, strictly by the utilization of thermals. Southbound migrants travel across the Kaibab Plateau, which provides plenty of cover for roosting and hunting. (Painted Desert to the east is avoided, perhaps because of its inhospitable conditions.) Many of the migrants seem to be guided by the narrow peninsulas of the North Rim that protrude into the canyon, and then head for northward-pointing fingers along the South Rim, such as Lipan and Yaki Points.

Observers stationed at these locations can get a good idea of the numbers of migratory raptors passing through the area. To get a "passage rate," counts are divided by the number of hours spent observing. For example, at Lipan Point, the passage rate has ranged from 1,107 to 1,957 raptors per 100 hours of observation. As many as 12,000 raptors were counted during one fall migration.

Sharp-shinned hawks, Cooper's hawks, red-tailed hawks, and American kestrels are the four most common species recorded. However, one observation that concerns the biologists is an apparent decrease in golden eagles.

Northern goshawks consume many small animals.

NORTHERN GOSHAWKS

In spite of commercial logging since the 1920s and private cutting before then, the Kaibab Plateau still has the most extensive tracts of old-growth ponderosa pine remaining in the Southwest. It's no coincidence that it also has the densest population of northern goshawks in North America. The Kaibab squirrel is one of this bird's favorite meals. Since the squirrel is wholly dependent upon ponderosa pine for food and shelter, there is a three-way relationship between the tree, the mammal, and the bird.

U.S. Forest Service researcher Richard Reynolds has spent decades studying goshawks on the Kaibab Plateau. His findings suggest that clumps of ponderosa pines interspersed with grassy areas not only make for ideal goshawk habitat but also provide perfect conditions for many other species. Reynolds believes that wildfire was the natural agent that maintained this type of forest structure.

Unfortunately, overgrazing by livestock, fire prevention, and heavy cutting of timber, especially old-growth trees, have upset this delicate balance. Reynolds hopes that his findings will help the forest service manage the forest in a more ecologically sustainable way in the future.

PEREGRINE FALCONS

Peregrine falcons are considered to be an indicator species, an index for the health of all plants and animals associated with them in the food chain. The first recorded sighting of a peregrine falcon on the North Rim was made by Florence Merriam Bailey in 1929. At that time, peregrines were considered "rare, casual visitors." In the May-June 1946 issue of *The Condor*, Richard Bond wrote, "[T]he tremendous cliffs of the Grand Canyon have not reported to harbor any eyries," yet today, at least 100 pairs nest within the park. Why the change?

In part, the "low" numbers of the early

1900s were possibly due to the difficulty in surveying such a large, rugged area and the scarcity of ornithologists. But Glen Canyon Dam's construction may also have played a role. After completion of the dam in 1963, the annual natural spring floods through the canyon and resultant scouring of the shoreline ceased.

Peregrine falcon dive at speeds of up to 200 miles (300 km) per hour.

Fairly quickly, vegetation began to claim the banks of the Colorado River. This new habitat spurred insect population growth, which in turn allowed the swift and swallow populations to increase. Additionally, more stable river flows apparently allowed an increase in waterfowl populations. The few peregrines in the neighborhood took advantage of these new avian food sources, and their reproduction increased. It's also possible that transient peregrines became canyon residents. Now, on average, there is a breeding pair of peregrines every three miles along the river.

CONDORS

The largest flying land bird in North America is once again soaring over the Grand Canyon region after nearly going extinct. California condors weigh up to twenty-six pounds and have a wingspan up to nine-and-a-half feet. Juveniles, which are as big as adults by the time they fledge, have dark-colored heads and black bills until they are three to four years old. They then develop a pinkish-orange, featherless head and ivory-colored bill. They may live to be sixty years old, but the females lay only a single egg every other year or so. Condors were once thought to be closely related to raptors, but DNA analysis has shown that storks are their closest relatives.

In prehistoric times, condors ranged from Canada to Mexico, and fossil evidence shows that condors have been nesting in the Grand Canyon region for at least 50,000 years. A dramatic decrease in their numbers occurred at the end of the last ice age, when many of their food sources—dead and decaying mastodons, giant ground sloths, and camels—disappeared. After the mid-1880s, Arizona had only scattered reports of condors. The last known active nest was near Lees Ferry in the 1890s. The last sighting of a condor in Arizona was near Williams in 1924. By 1982, only twenty-two condors remained in all of North America.

Through a captive breeding program, the condor population increased to nearly 300 birds by 2006. Reintroductions began in 1992 in California, 1996 in Arizona, and 2003 in Baja California, Mexico. Each bird is fitted with a radio transmitter and numbered wing tag before being released, and biologists monitor them daily.

California condors have nine-foot (3-m) wingspans.

After a hiatus of more than a century, condors are once again nesting in the Grand Canyon. During the spring of 2001, a condor laid an egg in a secluded cave near the North Rim. Unfortunately, the inexperienced parents broke it. Two years later, a chick managed to hatch and fledge; unfortunately, this young bird died in 2005, probably of malnutrition. Two more fledged in 2004. As of 2017, there were at least a dozen active nests in the Grand Canyon area. More than eighty condors now fly over northern Arizona. It has been a long, difficult struggle, but the survival of this unique creature in the wild seems assured.

COMMON RAVENS

The common raven is one of the most ubiquitous birds at the Grand Canyon, ranging from above the rim down to the Colorado River. Large flocks of ravens are sometimes seen in the meadows of the Kaibab Plateau, hopping about on the ground in search of grasshoppers and other insects. They are easily differentiated from crows (which are uncommon at the canyon) by their thick neck, shaggy throat feathers, and Bowie knife of a beak.

Considering their color and the color of most of the larger birds in sunny Arizona, doesn't it seem reasonable that birds out in the hot sun should be light in color, ideally white? Yet ravens are black, turkey vultures are dark brown, and most hawks also have dark feathers. The answer to this seemly contradictory situation is that the dark flight feathers absorb the radiant energy, while the underlying downy feathers insulate the body so heat is not transferred to the skin. Conversely, in arctic climes, animals are often white, which allows heat to pass more easily to their skin surface, which is usually dark.

Ravens appear solid black because their feathers reflect ultraviolet light.

Ravens and their corvid cousins (which include crows and jays) are considered to be among the geniuses of the bird world. They have been observed using sticks as tools, and have the ability to recognize individual humans and other animals. An acrobatic flier, ravens often do rolls and somersaults in the air. And, of course, they have quite a raucous vocabulary of squawks, calls, and croaks.

In addition to cavorting ravens, it is not unusual to see mixed flocks of violet-green swallows and white-throated swifts darting though the sky; their thin, pointed wings and high speed make them look like darts. Both species nest in tree cavities or in small holes in cliffs. Swifts, in particular, have very weak legs and almost never walk; they feed, drink, and even mate on the wing.

SNAGS, BIRDS, AND BATS

Snags—dead standing trees—are important homes to cavity-nesting animals. Tree swallows, bluebirds, northern flickers, hairy woodpeckers, white-breasted nuthatches, and pygmy nuthatches are some of the birds that require cavities. Snags are also an important habitat for the at least eighteen species of bats that occur in the Grand Canyon region, ranging from the tiny three-gram western pipistrelle to the fifty-seven-gram, two-foot-wingspan western mastiff bat.

Several of the typical forest-dwelling bats on the Kaibab Plateau include the myotis, big brown, Allen's lappet-browed,

An agile white-breasted nuthatch.

silver-haired, and hoary bat. A colony of dozens of bats may be located under the bark and in the crevices on a single snag. Each bat can consume 600 mosquitoes or other small insects per hour. A nursing little brown bat mother eats more than her body weight nightly, with her baby clinging to her in flight. During their nocturnal feeding flights, bats may cover 8,000 acres—astounding for such a tiny creature.

The bat's sonar, though impressively accurate for locating tiny insects, is not infallible. Park naturalist Eddie McKee witnessed two big brown bats colliding in midair. One fell into a water tank; the other landed on a rock.

LIZARDS

Nineteen or so species of lizards live in the Grand Canyon region. The small, light brown northern sagebrush lizard (*Sceloporus graciosus graciosus*) is the most common lizard in the North Rim forests, but also ranges down into piñon-juniper woodland. Adult males

Western bluebirds nest in tree cavities.

Plateau lizard

are marked with a pair of bright-blue belly patches and a throat mottled with blue. They feed on a variety of insects, including ants, beetles, termites, true bugs, and grasshoppers, and a variety of spiders and scorpions.

One lizard species has a most unusual way of procreating. The plateau striped whiptail (*Aspidoscelis velox*) only comes in the female gender. No males are known. During the breeding season, two females approach each other. One takes on the role of the male by doing push-up displays and head-bobbing. If that impresses the other lizard, she allows the male-acting one to mount her. It's all show, since no sperm is involved; however, the mating behavior apparently stimulates the submissive female's body to produce hormones that cause her unfertilized eggs to begin to grow into baby lizards. She lays three to five eggs in late June or early July, and they hatch several weeks later as genetic clones of their mother. This method of reproduction is called parthenogenesis and, while rare in vertebrates, is not uncommon in invertebrates.

GRAND CANYON RATTLESNAKES

One of the park's most famous, if not the most common, reptiles is the Grand Canyon rattlesnake, sometimes called the pink rattlesnake after one of its distinctive color variations. A variety of prairie rattlesnake, it is endemic to the canyon and has been christened with an appropriate Latin name: *Crotalus oreganus abyssus*, rattlesnake of the abyss. It occurs from Glen Canyon Dam downstream to National Canyon (river mile 166.5 left) and is rarely found above the rim. It was first collected by park naturalist Eddie McKee in 1929, and was described as a new subspecies by rattlesnake expert Laurence Klauber. Anecdotal evidence suggests that it is a rather mild-mannered snake, often refusing to rattle, let alone strike.

Several other species of rattlesnake are also found in the canyon: the southwestern speckled (*C. mitchellii pyrrhus*) and Mojave (*C. scutulatus scutulatus*) are known only from western Grand Canyon. The northern black-tailed rattlesnake (*C. molossus molossus*) is known from an old report as occurring in Havasu Canyon. The Great Basin rattlesnake (*C.*

Pink rattlesnakes locate prey with the help of a heat-sensing pit between their eyes and nostrils.

oreganus lutosus) occurs primarily on the north side of the canyon above the rim, while the Hopi rattlesnake (*C. organus nuntius*) lives mainly on the south side of the canyon above the rim. Biologists wonder about the exact genetic relationship between the three varieties of *Crotalus oreganus* where their ranges overlap. Could there be hybrids?

Then, there is the occasional rattlesnake mimic, the gopher snake. The Great Basin gopher snake (*Pituophis catenifer deserticola*) is harmless to humans. It does not have fangs nor is it poisonous. When frightened, the snake may coil its body, flatten its head to look more like the triangular rattlesnake head, and vibrate its tail. There are no rattles, but if there are dried leaves by the shaking tail, the sound can be unnerving.

NEOTENIC SALAMANDERS AND BROAD-HEADED CANNIBALS

The tiger salamander is Arizona's only salamander species. It has a remarkably wide distribution, ranging from boreal forest to desert. On the North Rim, the Utah tiger salamander (*Ambystoma tigrinum utahensis*) is found in pools in meadows and spruce-fir forests. Like other amphibians, it normally lays eggs in a pool of water, and they hatch into swimming larvae. Gradually, the larvae metamorphose into adult salamanders. However, in and around the small ponds located on the Kaibab Plateau, few adult tiger salamanders can be found. Yet, there are plenty of immature larval forms (neotonic) swimming in the water.

At high elevations, where temperatures are low and the summer growing season short, the tiger salamanders rarely change into true adult form. Miraculously, the neotonics may retain gills and other juvenile characteristics yet can become breeders and lay eggs.

There is one other odd fact about these salamanders: some are born as broad-headed cannibals while the rest are narrow-headed herbivores. Biologists are still trying to account for this strange phenomenon.

KANAB AMBERSNAIL

The isolated seeps and springs of Cliff Spring Trail sometimes harbor unique forms of plants and animals. During the last ice age when the region was much wetter, the ancestors of these water-loving organisms were widespread. But then as the Southwest became warmer and drier, only individuals that could find a watery refuge survived; over time, they evolved into endemic species or varieties. One such is the Kanab ambersnail.

Originally, this gastropod mollusk was known to exist in only two locations: on private land near Kanab, Utah, and at Vaseys Paradise, a lush, verdant spring gushing out of a cave in the Redwall Limestone at the edge of the Colorado River, deep within Marble Canyon. Scientists have made several transplants to other canyon springs in hopes of increasing the snail's chances of survival against the floodwaters periodically released by Glen Canyon Dam.

These dime-size mollusks are the intermediary host for a rare parasitic flatworm. As the snails eat the damp

52

vegetation, they ingest flatworm eggs.
The eggs hatch inside the snail, where
a single worm can grow to fill half of
the snail's body cavity. The worm then
pushes it neon-pink and green body
through the snail's eye sockets and
pulsates, which attracts the attention of
birds. The birds feed on the snails and
worms and excrete worm eggs, and the
cycle continues.

BUTTERFLIES

In the summertime, Kaibab Plateau
meadows are crisscrossed by butterflies
flitting from one flower to the next, feeding on sweet nectar. Poet Robert Frost
called them "flowers that fly, and all but
sing." Entomologists have a general rule
of thumb: insect diversity decreases as
elevation increases. But at the Grand
Canyon, the diversity of butterflies, and
their close relatives, the skippers, actually increases with altitude. Additionally,
there are four subspecies of butterflies
endemic to the park: scrub wood nymph
(*Cercyonis sthenele damei*), Grand
Canyon ringlet (*Coenonympha tullia
furcae*), Kaibab swallowtail (*Papilio indra
kaibabensis*), and Schellbach's Atlantis
fritillary (*Speyeria atlantis schellbachi*).

One of the greatest dangers to these
intrepid insects is the butterfly poacher.
The delicate Kaibab swallowtail has
been purchased on the black market for
$400 a pair. Perhaps that doesn't seem
like much of a problem, but consider
that this same illegal butterfly collector
bragged about going into the Rocky
Mountains and collecting 20,000 specimens on one trip. Then the seriousness

Kaibab swallowtail, flowers that fly.

becomes clear regarding the impact of
these unscrupulous individuals.

In 1934, David Rockefeller, Sr., then
a teenager, crossed the Grand Canyon
on a rim-to-rim hike with the canyon's
first major entomological-collecting
expedition. Fortunately, he deposited
specimens at Grand Canyon and several
other museums, including the American
Museum of Natural History in New York.
Rockefeller captured a southwestern
viceroy butterfly (*Limenitis archippus
obsoleta*) at Phantom Ranch, as well as
a number of aquatic beetles. He went
on to assemble the largest personal
beetle collection in the world. However,
the viceroy butterfly disappeared from
the Phantom Ranch area, and for many
decades was assumed to have been
extirpated from Grand Canyon. Then,
biologist Larry Stevens found viceroys
living in Deer Creek Valley in 2009,
confirming its continued existence in
Grand Canyon.

Geology

When geologists take in a landscape, two questions immediately come to mind: What is the origin of the various rock layers, and how were these deposits shaped into the present landscape? For the Grand Canyon, the answers to these two questions are long and complex, and details are still being determined.

There are three basic groups of rocks: sedimentary (layered deposits), igneous (born of fire), and metamorphic (formed under heat and pressure). The Grand Canyon's oldest exposed rocks are down by the river, although the range within that simple statement is astoundingly great. In this relatively open part of the canyon, the oldest rocks are 1.2 billion years old. Just a few miles downstream, the river cuts into an even older layer, the Vishnu Schist and related granites, that is about 1.8 billion years old.

Those colorful, soft-looking slopes and ledges are the remnants of a mountain range that once covered northern Arizona. Sediments and lavas were laid down over millions of years to an accumulated depth of more than 12,000 feet (3,658 m), or a total of 2 vertical miles (3.2 km). Then, these deposits were stretched during the splitting-apart of a supercontinent—an effect of plate tectonics. The rock split along faults and then tilted into a huge mountain range. As time passed, these gigantic mountains were worn down until they were almost totally erased. Only remnants remain, some which can be seen in a few places within the Grand Canyon.

Eventually, a sea encroached from the west, drowning the region but also setting up the conditions for sands to be deposited near the shoreline. Finer clays were carried farther out to sea and deposited; beyond, in the clear, warm water, corals began to grow. As the shoreline slowly shifted to the east,

Granite dikes and sills in schist.

Colorado River at Unkar Rapids amid Grand Canyon Series rocks.

these three different depositional zones also shifted eastward. Today, we see Tapeats Sandstone, Bright Angel Shale, and Muav Limestone as products of this ancient Cambrian time.

As the Cambrian sea retreated, another one encroached, and the massive Redwall Limestone was the result. Environmental conditions changed again and again—more oceans, times of desert sands, swampy periods punctuated by droughts, more seas. Millions upon millions of years passed. Then, about 80 million years ago, the geologic story shifted once more from deposition to erosion. Layers laid down during the Mesozoic—the Age of Reptiles—were carried away by water and wind and time, leaving the Permian Kaibab Limestone as the future rim of the Grand Canyon.

This leads to the next question: How did this magnificent landform come to be? The final answer is still being debated. The oversimplified explanation? The river did it.

Geologists do agree that the river (or maybe more than one river) is responsible for carving the depths of the Grand Canyon. The widening of the canyon can be explained by erosion and weathering of rocks by rain, freeze/thaw activity, and chemical action. Gravity pulled all the fragments downward to the river, which attempted to carry the debris away.

But, as mentioned, the details, including the age of the canyon, are still being sorted out. Competing evolving theories are excellently described in geologist Wayne Ranney's book, *Carving Grand Canyon: Evidence, Theories, and Mystery.*

People and Places

THE CANYON'S ORIGINAL PEOPLE

Near the end of the last ice age, a Paleo-Indian hunter dropped his stone spear point in the Nankoweap basin below Point Imperial. Eleven thousand years later, in 1993, an archaeologist discovered a fragment of this broken Folsom-style point.

For thousands of years, other hunters and gatherers traveled through this section of the Grand Canyon, leaving behind tantalizing bits of evidence—perhaps a split-twig figurine or enigmatic pictograph. Beginning about 2,500 years ago, families built small stone houses and began to plant maize in the Grand Canyon region. Twelve hundred years later, they grew cotton along with beans and squash, storing their harvest in granaries tucked into the cliffs and living in small above-ground masonry houses. Hunting was still an important part of their lives, as well as gathering medicinal plants and wild foods in season, such as piñon nuts, cactus fruits, and grass seeds.

After several centuries of relatively stable living conditions, something caused the people to leave their canyon homes. Where did they go? Probably toward the east to become the ancestors of the Hopi and other Pueblo peoples. Different groups came to live in the area, among them, the Hualapai, Havasupai, Southern Paiute, and Navajo. Exactly when these other people began to occupy the Grand Canyon region is debated, but they have been here for at least hundreds of years.

Ancestral Puebloans

The Ancestral Puebloans, previously referred to as the Anasazi, are the prehistoric inhabitants of the Four Corners region of the Southwest. The word "Anasazi" is a corruption of a Navajo word that approximates to "enemy ancestors" or "ancient others," and in many ways is an apt description, since the Navajo and Pueblo people have a history of discord. Nonetheless, the word has negative connotations, and in the past decades, an increasing number of modern Pueblo tribes have objected to the use of a Navajo word to describe their ancestors.

Split-twig figurine

In 1949, Douglas W. Schwartz, a graduate student in archaeology, made his first visit to the Grand Canyon. He assumed, like other archaeologists of the time, that the inner canyon and the raging Colorado River were too inhospitable for large populations of prehistoric farmers. But thirty years of fieldwork radically changed his thinking. After several archaeological surveys throughout the canyon, he and his assistants conducted extensive pioneering excavations in three areas: Unkar Delta, Walhalla Plateau, and Bright Angel Pueblo, a small site along the Colorado River near Bright Angel Creek. Continuing archaeological studies have revealed a very long human presence in the Grand Canyon and surrounding region, one that stretches back some 13,000 years.

Starting about AD 850, the Ancestral Puebloan people lived on the Unkar Delta and along Unkar Creek. There they grew corn, beans, squash, and perhaps cotton, and built small stone houses to live in and kivas (underground rooms) for ceremonies. By AD 1200, Unkar and most other inner canyon settlements had been abandoned. The reasons for this are not clear, but there is some evidence that the climate became cooler and drier, which would have had a detrimental effect on crops.

Near the Walhalla Plateau, the Kaibab Limestone is somewhat sandy and easily breaks into blocks and slabs that are useful for building structures. Chert inclusions offer a prime source of raw material for stone tools. Finely crafted axe heads were made for felling trees. (By contrast, only poorly made axes have been found at Unkar. Not surprising, since driftwood was available along the river, hence no need for an ax.) Water was probably always scarce on the plateau, but small springs and sinkhole ponds may have been more reliable than they are today.

Life was far from easy. The people were plagued with periodontal disease, tooth abscesses, and osteoarthritis. The dead were often buried with pottery vessels and bracelets of shale and turquoise beads, possibly indicating a belief in an afterlife.

EARLY VISITORS AND NOTABLE FIRSTS

Although nineteenth-century Mormon scout Jacob Hamblin was one of first European Americans recorded on the north side of the Grand Canyon, there may have been other early visitors. Burly, six-foot, four-inch trapper Joe Walker declared that he would raft the canyons of the Colorado River from Wyoming to the Mohave villages in western Arizona. Very few mountain men were literate, and those who were rarely ever wrote about their travels, especially if they were trespassing. Some historians believe that Walker may have trapped along Bright Angel Creek in the early 1840s, when the territory was still under Mexican rule. Trapper and scout Jedediah S. Smith left an inscription at House Rock Spring at the base of the Vermilion Cliffs dated September 21 but no year. It is, however, known that he was in southwest Utah in 1826 and 1827.

John Wesley Powell

In 1861, during the early days of the Civil War, an intense, largely self-taught,

John Wesley Powell and Paiute Chief Tau-Gu, ca. 1873.

twenty-seven-year-old public-school principal from Illinois, John Wesley Powell, joined the Union Army. The next spring, at Shiloh, as Powell raised his right arm to signal a barrage, a Confederate minié ball shattered the bone in his arm, requiring amputation. Undaunted, Powell continued to serve until almost the end of the Civil War. Once the war ended, he taught courses in botany, zoology, anatomy, entomology, and geology at Illinois Wesleyan University.

The summers of 1867 and 1868 were spent in the Rockies with his wife Emma and a small crew of students and relatives, exploring and studying the upper reaches of the Colorado River. Powell hoped to "shed light on the central forces that formed the continent." This goal eventually led to a plan to explore the large blank area that appeared on the best maps of the time. He would descend the Green River to its junction with the Grand (years later, the state of Colorado had the Grand River's name changed to Colorado) and continue down the Colorado. He would flesh out the terra incognito.

Powell took advantage of the nation's first and recently completed transcontinental railroad to have four wooden boats of his design shipped to Green River Station, Wyoming Territory. On May 24, 1869, Powell and his nine-man crew of volunteers pushed off. Rapids quickly extracted their toll. A boat, gear, and food were lost, and one man was left near Vernal, Utah. On August 10, they arrived at the mouth of the Little Colorado River, deep within the Grand Canyon, and the beginning of what Powell called the "Great Unknown." Little did they realize how difficult the rapids ahead would be. Endless days dragged on as the men toiled with the heavy boats, navigating what rapids they could, often lining (walking on shore, hanging onto the boat with lines, and letting the current carry the craft) or carrying the boats around unrunnable cascades. Food was running short, and what they had left was moldy.

After three months on the river, they came upon yet another horrendous rapid—this time with no way to walk around it. Three men had had enough of the river and of Powell's arrogant, aloof leadership. They hiked out through what is now called Separation Canyon and were never seen again. As it turned out, this was almost the last rapid. The next day, August 30, Powell and the remaining five men emerged from the Grand Canyon.

Powell's exploits made him a national hero. He would return to the river in 1871–1872 better funded and with the previous trip's experience behind him, to study the Grand Canyon region's geology and indigenous people. Powell went on to become a powerful bureaucrat in Washington, D.C., eventually becoming the second director of the U.S. Geological Survey and heading up the Smithsonian's Bureau of American Ethnology. He was also a founding member of the National Geographic Society.

Ellen Powell Thompson

In the early 1870s, when John Wesley Powell was putting together a team to carry out a survey of southern Utah and northern Arizona, he chose his sister's husband, Almon Harris Thompson, to fill in the white space on Lt. G. W. Warren's 1857 Pacific railroad survey map. Thompson became chief geographer of the newly formed United States Geological Survey and also helped create a group to promote geographical knowledge, which later became the National Geographic Society.

Thompson explored southern Utah and the Arizona Strip from 1872 to 1875. With him was his wife, Ellen "Nellie" Powell Thompson. She had been trained in botany at Wheaton College, and while her husband mapped, she collected plants. Nellie accompanied the Powell Survey onto the Kaibab Plateau, where she collected a number of plants new to science. Occasionally, she would stay behind to work on her plant collections, living in a tent in Jacob Hamblin's Kanab, Utah, yard with her dog, Fuzz. Nellie also has the distinction of being the first woman to boat through a Grand Canyon rapid, the Paria riffle near Lees Ferry in 1872. Perhaps not surprisingly, this strong, self-sufficient woman later became a nationally known suffragette.

Buffalo Bill Cody

While representing the Church of Jesus Christ of Latter-day Saints (AKA LDS or Mormons) in England, John W. Young, one of church leader Brigham Young's sons, conceived a scheme for turning the Kaibab Plateau into a hunting ground. Among the attractions he proposed were free-ranging African lions and Asian big-game animals, and making it a center for tourist recreation, complete with hotels and lodges for English nobility. Coincidentally, Buffalo Bill Cody was in England with his Wild West Show. Young approached him and proposed that Cody

Buffalo Bill (second from right) and party with local guide John Hance (far right), 1892.

come to the Kaibab and act as guide for two English lords, Colonel W.H. MacKinnon and Major St. John Mildmay.

The Cody party arrived at the South Rim in the summer of 1892. After being shown around by legendary prospector-turned-tour guide John Hance, Cody and the prospective hunters followed the primitive trail around the eastern flank of the Grand Canyon and then north to Lees Ferry, crossed the river, and continued to the Kaibab Plateau.

From the Kaibab, the party visited Kanab, where they had dinner with Uncle Dee Woolley and his wife, Emma. After the meal, Buffalo Bill praised Emma, saying, "God bless the hands that made them custard pies." Though well treated, the British lords decided the plateau's game was too far from England and much too difficult to reach.

François Emile Matthes

The first topographic map of the Grand Canyon, arguably one of the finest maps ever made, was the masterpiece of François Emile Matthes, with the U.S. Geological Survey. In the summer of 1902, he began mapping on the South Rim. When it became time to move to the North Rim, he was assured that Bright Angel Canyon was impassable. So Matthes and his men decided to use the rugged Bass Trail, about twenty miles to the west. At the river, they discovered that Bass's boat was on the north side. Matthes and another man swam the dangerous river to retrieve the boat. Their

Matthes mapping the canyon, 1904.

horses and mules were reluctant to cross but were pushed into the water. The entire canyon crossing took six days.

While mapping the canyon's buttes, mesas, and other formations, Matthes decided to continue applying the "heroic nomenclature," which he incorrectly thought was begun by John Wesley Powell. It was actually geologist Charles Dutton who started the practice in the 1880s. Matthes added names such as Krishna Shrine, Solomon Temple, Wotans Throne, and Walhalla Plateau to his map.

As summer waned and winter approached, the survey team decided to see if Bright Angel Canyon was indeed impassable. They were startled to encounter "two haggard men and a weary burro" emerging from the depths. Matthes and his crew roughed out a trail down Bright Angel Canyon to the river that was "so steep…that the animals fairly slid down on their haunches. So narrow between the rocks was it at one point that the larger packs could not pass through and had to be unloaded."

They forded Bright Angel Creek ninety-four times. At the river, a prospector loaned them his boat for the crossing.

Uncle Dee Woolley

In 1903, prominent Kanab resident Edwin Dilworth "Uncle Dee" Woolley formed the Grand Canyon Transportation Company, which included a plan to provide a cross-canyon route for tourists. By 1906, Matthes's "trail" had been improved by Woolley's son-in-law, David Rust, and his crew. The following year, a cable with a cage was strung across the Colorado River near the mouth of Bright

Left to right: Woolley, Utah Senator Sutherland, and Utah Governor Thomas on North Rim, 1905.

Angel Creek. Big enough for one mule, the cage was suspended from the cable on pulleys and pulled back and forth using a lighter cable.

Uncle Dee and his nephew Gordon sponsored the first attempt to drive an automobile from Salt Lake City via Kanab to the North Rim. In June 1909, a Locomobile and a Thomas Flyer made the journey from Kanab in three days. The vehicles only got three miles per gallon, so gasoline was cached along the way. Passengers had to do road repair as they went along. The autos wore out nine tires, which were later exhibited by the U.S. Rubber Company to demonstrate their durability. Needless to say, there wasn't a rush of auto traffic to the North Rim after this expedition. The wagon road from Kanab to Bright Angel Point was upgraded for automobiles in 1913.

Rust established a utilitarian tourist tent camp near the mouth of Bright Angel Creek. He dug irrigation ditches and planted cottonwoods and various fruit trees. After Theodore Roosevelt spent time here in 1913 on his way to the North Rim to hunt, Rust's Camp became known as Roosevelt's Camp. By 1922, Rust's old camp was superseded by the construction of Phantom Ranch, which offered comfortable cabins, a lodge, and a canteen.

Pearl Zane Gray

In 1906, Pearl Gray, a struggling author whose daytime job was dentistry, attended a lecture given by Charles Jesse "Buffalo" Jones, describing his cattalo (offspring of bison and domestic cows) experiments and roping mountain lions at the Grand Canyon. While most of the audience was

Author Zane Grey

incredulous, Pearl was riveted by these tales. Introductions were forthcoming and plans were laid.

The next spring, Pearl stepped off the train in Flagstaff, where Jones was waiting for him. They rode horseback north along the base of the Echo Cliffs, crossed the Colorado River at Lees Ferry, and continued to Jones's ranch, where Pearl photographed one of the cattalos.

Eventually, it was time to ride up onto the Kaibab Plateau and to a detached sky-island within the Grand Canyon known as the Powell Plateau. Jones proclaimed that the isolated Powell Plateau was the breeding ground for hundreds of lions that "infest the North Rim of the canyon," and that no "white man or Indian" had ever hunted lions there.

The party used dogs to track, chase, and eventually tree a lion. Then Jones and the others lassoed the terrified critter while trying to stay clear of the cat's sharp claws and teeth. The lion's feet were tied, claws clipped, and mouth muzzled. Six lions were captured alive, several were killed, and many escaped. Pearl was amazed.

After returning home, Pearl fired off several articles, stories, and a book, *The Last of the Plainsmen*, based on his Grand Canyon adventures. The reading public began to take notice of this new author, who changed the spelling of his surname from Gray to Grey and dropped his effeminate first name in favor of his manlier middle one: Zane.

Zane Grey eventually wrote more than ninety books, which have sold more than forty million copies. *Riders of the Purple Sage* was (and still is) his best seller. More than one hundred movies and television programs have been based on his works.

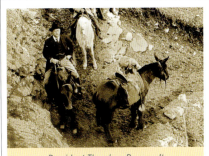

President Theodore Roosevelt

Theodore Roosevelt

After losing the 1912 presidential election to Woodrow Wilson, Theodore Roosevelt planned a hunting trip on the Kaibab Plateau. His sons Quentin and Archie and cousin Nicholas were invited. The hunt would be followed by a pack trip to the recently "discovered" Rainbow Bridge, near the foot of Navajo Mountain for the following year. Dave Rust, an outfitter from Kanab, would provide a guide, packer, cook, wrangler, pack outfit, and riding stock.

Nicholas was to make the arrangements. T.R. wrote to him to be sure to include "15 pounds coffee, some tea… ample supply of frijoles, some jerky, dried fruit (not prunes), thirty cans of sardines and a supply of Borden's condensed milk."

T.R., Archie, and Quentin arrived at the South Rim on the Santa Fe Railway's "California Limited." After spending the night of July 14, 1913, at the El Tovar Hotel, the Roosevelt party climbed aboard Fred Harvey mules to descend the Bright Angel Trail to the Colorado River. Following the Roosevelt Party down the trail was Henry S. Stephenson, "the boss" of the Bar Z, one of the largest cattle operations on the Kaibab Plateau. As a thunderstorm boomed above them, they took turns crossing the river in Rust's caged cable car, pulled slowly by an old man, who turned out to be the foreman of the Bar Z Ranch.

But Rust's people were not there (they had the wrong meeting date), so T.R. decided to throw in with Stephenson and use his guide, government hunter and game warden Jim "Uncle Jimmy" Owens. Owens declared, "We'll eat off the land—mountain lion meat and wild horse flesh!" Although T.R. found Owens, a transplanted Texan, "to be diffident with a sad air, almost illiterate, he had the manners of a gentleman and was free from spite and malice." They spent two weeks hunting on the North Rim before continuing to northeastern Arizona to visit Rainbow Bridge, only the tenth party to do so since the natural bridge's discovery in 1909.

Pauline Patraw

In 1927, Pauline "Polly" Mead was a twenty-three-year-old botany student at the University of Chicago when she made a summer-long field trip to the West, which included a visit to the Grand Canyon. After she set up camp in the Kaibab forest, her professor, Dr. Henry Cowles, suggested that she stroll through the trees and take a look at the canyon. "I walked down the path and discovered the Grand Canyon. A most emotional experience. It was so wonderful," she wrote.

Later, as the group was leaving the Kaibab Plateau, Dr. Cowles pointed out how the trees came to the edge of a meadow and suddenly stopped. He wondered out loud why that was so. Polly decided to investigate that question as her master's thesis. She spent the next two summers near the North Rim doing her research, which expanded into the first complete study of plant life on the Kaibab.

Pauline Patraw, Grand Canyon's first female ranger-naturalist.

After graduation, Polly wanted to remain at the canyon. She applied for a job with the U.S. Forest Service; when she was informed that the agency didn't hire women, she applied to the National Park Service. Polly was sworn in on August 1, 1930, by the park's assistant superintendent, Preston Patraw. She was the first female ranger-naturalist at Grand Canyon, and only the second in the entire National Park Service. Since there was no official ranger uniform for women, the superintendent decided that she should wear a riding habit topped off with "a hat like the courier girls for Fred Harvey tours wore."

Later, Patraw invited Polly to accompany him on a hike up Red Butte, near the South Rim. Love bloomed in the spring of 1931, and they were married in May. Though Preston was transferred to several other parks, the Patraws ended up back at the Grand Canyon in 1954, when he was appointed superintendent. Polly had returned to her canyon home.

And why did the trees stop at the meadow's edge? Polly's answer was that the meadow's soils were too high in lime content for the trees. Subsequent studies seem to indicate that the meadows are too wet in the spring for most of the seedlings, causing them to rot; hot, dry summer temperatures then kill any that do manage to germinate. More recently, researchers have shown that the Kaibab meadows have been decreasing in size since the mid-1930s, and most dramatically since the 1970s, as aspens invade the meadow areas, perhaps due to fire suppression and a century of regional warming.

Rose Collom

In 1932, park residents organized the Grand Canyon Natural History Association (today's Grand Canyon Conservancy) to help offset decreased park service appropriations for visitor education, interpretation, and research. As one of its initial acts, the GCNHA funded the park's first botanist, Rose Collom. From

Rose Collom collecting plants on the North Rim, ca. 1940s.

the mid-1930s until the 1950s, Collom worked primarily on plant checklists and collections, and maintained an herbarium. She discovered several new species of plants, including a delicate buttercup (*Ranunculus oreogenes*) that blossoms in moist areas of the North Rim. Collom also encouraged the use of native Arizona plants for landscaping in home gardens and beside highways.

Eddie McKee

Eddie McKee, the "premier research scientist of Grand Canyon geology."

In 1964, geologist and former chief park naturalist Edwin McKee organized the "Symposium on the Cenozoic Geology of the Colorado Plateau in Arizona." The prosaic title gave little hint to the general public of what the scientists were up to: coming together to figure out how the Grand Canyon was formed.

McKee had a long association with the canyon. As a Boy Scout in Washington, D.C., his troop leader was François

Emile Matthes, who in 1902 had made the first topographic maps of the Grand Canyon. Twenty-five years later, Matthes arranged for McKee (by then, a geology student at the Naval Academy) to intern with paleontologist John C. Merriam, president of the Carnegie Institution of Washington, who was developing programs for Grand Canyon National Park.

In February 1929, after park naturalist Glen Sturdevant drowned while attempting to cross the Colorado River, McKee was appointed to take his place. At the canyon, McKee met and fell in love with a biologist named Barbara Hastings. However, there was literally a chasm between them. She worked on the North Rim, he was stationed on the South. But Eddie didn't let a twenty-five-mile hike—one way—interfere with his courting, and on the last day of 1929, they wed.

While McKee's 1964 symposium didn't answer the question of the origin of the Grand Canyon, it did stimulate new theories and more research. The search for the answer continues today. Modern geological science, which is only a few centuries old, is attempting to answer million-year-old mysteries. Within just the last five decades, major revelations in the nature of the Earth's geological functions have inspired new paradigms: plate tectonics; the evolution of river systems over time; and at the Grand Canyon, that the history of the rocks and the history of the river and its canyon are separate stories.

Approaching Nankoweap, *oil on canvas, 2005*

Bruce Aiken

As a child growing up among the concrete canyons of New York City, Bruce Aiken dreamed of living at the end of a long dirt road. Incredibly, his wish was realized in 1973 when he was hired to work and live at the Roaring Springs pump house along the North Kaibab Trail, deep within the canyon. For more than thirty years, Aiken tended the machinery that pumped water to the North Rim. He and his wife, Mary, raised three children in this remote spot. Grocery shopping was a two-day affair. They made do by baking bread, raising a small garden, collecting watercress for salads, and fishing in Bright Angel Creek.

Aiken is also an artist. As a teen, he trained at New York City's Art Students League, and later at the School of Visual Arts in Manhattan. He initially found the Grand Canyon too overwhelming to capture on canvas, but as he studied and came to know his new home, he began to sketch, then painted small canvases. Over time, he tackled larger and larger painting projects and is now recognized as one of the great artistic interpreters of the Grand Canyon and its many moods and secrets.

In 2006, after more than three decades of living below the rim, Bruce and Mary decided that it was time to retire from the canyon and seek new horizons. The pump house is now controlled by a computerized system.

PIONEER TOURISM

A Tent Camp and a Burro Named Brighty

Elizabeth Wylie McKee and her husband, Thomas, opened a tourist camp near Bright Angel Point in 1917. This was one of the earliest tourist facilities on the North Rim. By this time, the South Rim had been quite developed, with several hotels (including the elegant El Tovar),

Wylie Camp cabins, 1926.

mule rides, and interpretive lectures. It is important to remember that the Santa Fe Railroad had arrived at the South Rim in 1901, allowing visitors to reach the canyon in relative comfort. Reaching the

North Rim was not so easy.

Earlier in 1917, Elizabeth's brothers, Fred and Clinton, became lost attempting to reach Bright Angel Point in their Model T roadster. They ran out of gas but were rescued by a sheepherder, who eventually towed them back to town two weeks later.

In spite of the difficulties, the Union Pacific Railroad envisioned the building of similarly upscale tourist facilities at Bryce Canyon, Zion, and the North Rim. The railroad invited Elizabeth's father, William Wallace Wylie, to start primitive camps at Zion and the North Rim, as he had done in Yellowstone National Park. If these camps worked out, the railroad would invest in resort accommodations.

William Wylie originated what became known as the "Wylie Way" camp concept. This consisted of a central services building surrounded by tent-cabins. The tent-cabins had wooden floors and walls to a height of four feet, topped by three-foot walls and roofs of striped canvas. The cabins were partitioned with sheets into several rooms, nicely furnished, and heated with a Sibley stove. Guided trips were offered, and lectures and entertainment filled the evenings.

While William established a camp in Zion, his daughter and son-in-law went to the North Rim. It was tough going. Firewood had to be collected and split. Water had to be hauled from a spring below the rim in Transept Canyon. Fortunately, a friendly gelded burro named Bright Angel helped with that task.

By 1926, North Rim visitation had increased to 14,500, and the camp showed promise of turning a good profit. However, the Union Pacific and the National Park Service decided it was now time for real development. The McKees were forced to sell out during the 1927 season as the Grand Canyon Lodge was being built, marking the end of the pioneer era of tourism at the North Rim. Although regional boosters repeatedly tried to get the railroad to build a line to the North Rim and Bryce and Zion, the closest rail lines ever established were spurs to Marysvale and Cedar City, in Utah.

Thomas and Elizabeth McKee (left), Wylie Camp proprietors from 1917 to 1926, with their son, camp workers, and Brighty the burro.

In the June 1921 issue of *National Geographic Magazine*, geographer Harriet Chalmers Adams wrote, "Here [at that time Roosevelt camp, now Phantom Ranch] we discover the bridge mascot, Little Bright Angel, a gray burro who lives in Elysian Fields, with clear water, plenty of grass, and a care-free life. We fed him pancakes sent by the cook, his favorite dish.

"There are 113 crossings of the creek on the trail up Bright Angel Canyon to the North Rim, and the little burro knows every one of them. Not long ago he guided the foreman of the bridge-crew up to the plateau, showing him just where to cross the stream."

Children's author Marguerite Henry wrote a number of classic horse stories, but only one had a burro as the main character. Her Newbery Award–winning *Brighty of the Grand Canyon* was based on real people, animals, and events, including a fictionalized account of Teddy Roosevelt's 1913 cougar-hunting trip with Jim Owens. As Henry concludes, "[I]t is trail dust out of the past, kicked up by Brighty himself, the roving spirit of the Grand Canyon—forever wild, forever free."

Grand Canyon Lodge

Grand Canyon Lodge seems to grow directly out of the canyon's limestone rim. Early visitors typically arrived in a White Motor Company Bus and were greeted by college-age employees singing a welcome at the entrance. Architect Gilbert Stanley Underwood designed the rustic building so that visitors would be "surprised" by the view of the Grand Canyon as they entered the front doors, crossed the lobby, and then descended into the Sun Room, which faces the abyss.

However, the lodge seen today is not the first one, which was completed in 1928. The first lodge was commissioned by the then-concessionaire to the North Rim, the Utah Parks Company, a wholly owned subsidiary of the Union Pacific Railroad. Though Steven Mather, the first director of the National Park Service, requested a rustic design, Underwood's

Grand Canyon Lodge

original building included a massive Spanish-style exterior with a high front capped by an observation tower. A crew worked through the winter of 1927–1928 to complete the lodge and its attendant cabins. The following summer, the lodge opened for business.

Tragically, in the early morning hours of September 1, 1932, a fire broke out below the kitchen and quickly spread. Within minutes, the structure was engulfed in flames. The lodge manager, his wife, and the maids were able to escape but watched helplessly as fire consumed the building. Fortunately, all but two of the nearby tourist cabins escaped the blaze.

The Utah Parks Company quickly erected a cafeteria and recreation hall, but it was 1937 before a new lodge was completed atop the foundation of the original. The present lodge has sloped

Brighty of the Grand Canyon, sculpted by Peter Jepson.

roofs to shed the heavy winter snows and no tower, but retains the "surprise view" in the Sun Room.

Soft, brown-leather sofas provide resting spots to gaze through the giant picture windows that frame a panoramic view of the canyon. This is also a wonderful, and safe, place to witness the fury of an afternoon thunderstorm sweeping across the gorge. In one corner, a limestone-edged fireplace adds warmth and cheer on cool summer evenings or chilly autumn days. A statue of Brighty, the canyon's most famous burro, is nearby. The burro's nose is polished to a shine by the countless hands that have rubbed it for good luck.

The Colorado River is not visible from the lodge, but no matter. The vast, unfolding scene is more than enough to invoke awe. And across the great gorge, beyond the South Rim, is the horizon,

Cabins at Phantom Ranch.

studded with the numerous volcanoes and cinder cones of the San Francisco Volcanic Field, evidence of the area's more recent geologic activity.

To celebrate the wonderful dark night sky, star parties are held each summer, when telescope viewing is offered on the lodge terrace.

Phantom Ranch

Phantom Ranch, which replaced the ramshackle Roosevelt Camp formerly known as Rust's Camp, opened in November 1922. Until World War II, the ranch was a rather exclusive hideaway, attracting the wealthy and famous. Today, it is a sought-after overnight destination for hikers going from the North Rim to the South Rim (and vice versa), or from one rim down and back.

The ranch was expanded several times over the years. During 1927–1928, eight more guest cabins were constructed, the dining hall enlarged, and a recreation building added. During the Civilian Conservation Corps years of 1933–1942, a naturalistic pond-shaped swimming pool was built. Water from Bright Angel Creek flowed in one end and out the opposite. (Unfortunately, in 1972, new public hygiene regulations couldn't be met, and the pool was filled in.)

The CCC boys (Company 818) were stationed downstream of Phantom Ranch during the winter months; their campsite eventually became Bright Angel Campground. They built a spur trail to Upper Ribbon Falls and the nine-mile trail to Clear Creek. A 1935 advertisement promoted a mule ride from Phantom Ranch to Clear Creek to enjoy the excellent fishing and visits to "Indian ruins." The boys of Company 818 also constructed the River Trail that runs along the south side of the Colorado River to connect the Bright Angel and South Kaibab Trails.

View from above Phantom Ranch.

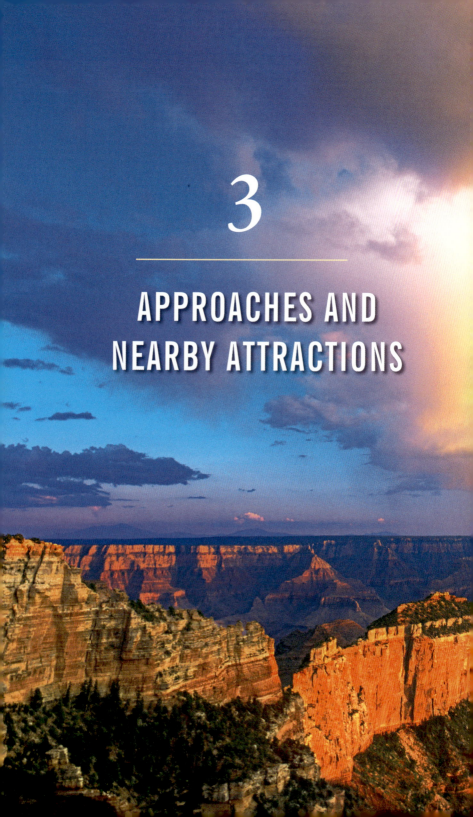

3

APPROACHES AND NEARBY ATTRACTIONS

to St. George
to Panguitch
to KANAB
COLORADO CITY
UTAH
ARIZONA
389
FREDONIA
89A
KAIBAB PAIUTE INDIAN RES.
89A
VERMILION CLIFFS NAT. MON. AND WILDERNESS
LE FE
PIPE SPRING NAT. MON.
89A
ARIZONA STRIP
JACOB LAKE
67
Kaibab National Forest
NAVAJO INDIAN RES.
MT. TRUMBULL WILDERNESS
DeMotte Park
North Rim Entrance Station
GRAND CANYON NATIONAL PARK
Toroweap Overlook
Bright Angel Point
HAVASUPAI INDIAN RES.
HUALAPAI INDIAN RES.
South Rim
Grand Canyon Village

N
W E
S
0   5   10 miles
0   8   16 km

Kaibab National Forest

ARIZONA STRIP
AS SEEN FROM SPACE

Grand Wash Cliffs
SHIVWITS PLATEAU
UINKARET PLATEAU
KANAB PLATEAU
GRAND CANYON
KAIBAB PLATEAU
PARIA PLATEAU
Vermilion Cliffs
MARBLE PLATFORM
Colorado River
COCONINO PLATEAU

The Arizona Strip

Sharlot Hall and Al Doyle prepare to cross the Colorado River, 1911.

Topographically, the Arizona Strip can be broken into seven major subdivisions: Marble Platform; the Paria, Kaibab, Kanab, Uinkaret, and Shivwits Plateaus, all subdivisions of the greater Colorado Plateau; and a slice of Basin and Range country. Going west along the base of the Paria Plateau from the Colorado River (entrenched deep in Marble Canyon), Marble Platform's relatively flat desert rises likes a giant cresting wave to become the high, forested Kaibab Plateau. Marble Platform is bounded on the north by the southern escarpment of the Paria Plateau—the spectacular Vermilion Cliffs.

On the west side of the Kaibab, the land drops back into arid country in a series of dramatic steps to form the Kanab, Uinkaret, and Shivwits Plateaus. The far west side of the Shivwits drops off into the Grand Wash Cliffs, marking the edge of the Colorado Plateau region and the beginning of the lower deserts and corrugated mountains of the Basin and Range Province.

Technically, the region typically thought of as the North Rim is the southern extension of the Kaibab Plateau. The name "Kaibab" is generally translated as "mountain lying down," an apt description of the high plateau, which is relatively flat on top. Kaibab is likely derived from the corruption of the Southern Paiute word *Kaivavitsets*, which refers to the Mountain Lying Down People (or Kaibab Paiute People). Early pioneers usually called the plateau Buckskin Mountain, referencing the numerous mule deer that lived there. However, Frederick Dellenbaugh, one of explorer and geologist John Wesley Powell's men, thought the Buckskin name was derived from the plateau's resemblance to a skin stretched out on the ground. Regardless of the exact origin of its name, the Kaibab Plateau is indeed a "mountain lying down," covered with a beautiful forest and alive with deer and other wildlife.

Only a few small towns and scattered ranches exist on the vast Arizona Strip: Colorado City, famous—or perhaps notorious—as a polygamist community; Moccasin, on the Kaibab Indian Reservation; Fredonia, a quiet, friendly ranching outpost and, with about 1,300 residents, the largest town on the Strip; and Littlefield, a farming community along I-15. (Marble Canyon, Vermilion Cliffs, Cliff Dwellers, Kaibab Lodge, and Jacob Lake are all too small to qualify as towns but do offer lodging, meals, and a few basic services, at least seasonally.)

A LAND MADE FOR EXPLORATION

The Grand Canyon is an effective barrier between most of Arizona and the northwest corner of the state—the Arizona Strip. While the Strip is politically connected to Arizona, geographically and historically, it is more aligned with Utah.

Back in 1911, when Arizona was still a territory, Utah attempted to acquire the Strip. That same year, Arizona poet, travel writer, and historian Sharlot Hall, along with Flagstaff guide Allen Doyle, set out on a daring, two-month-long

Venturing Off-Pavement: A Warning!

While there are many sites on the remote Arizona Strip that are worth exploring, do not leave the paved highway unless you are sure that the roads are passable and that you have appropriate maps, available at forest service and Bureau of Land Management visitor centers. Do not rely on GPS! High-clearance vehicles with two full-size spare tires, food, and water are strongly recommended. There are no services once you leave the pavement, and cell phone reception is unreliable.

journey to explore the area, record its natural resources, talk to its residents, and chronicle its history. With two fine Arabian ponies drawing a Studebaker wagon, Hall and Doyle left Flagstaff on July 23 and made their way north toward Tuba City and Lees Ferry on a dirt road that roughly paralleled today's U.S. Highway 89.

The road dropped down from the cool ponderosa pine forest into the warmer and drier piñon-juniper woodland, which was slowly replaced by grasslands, and finally entered the stark Painted Desert and Navajo country. It took them two days just to reach the banks of the Little Colorado River, which was in flood following summer thunderstorms. Fortunately, a mining outfit headed by Charles Spencer was also attempting to cross and helped them out.

Hall and Doyle bought additional supplies at Preston's Trading Post in Tuba City before continuing north along the base of Echo Cliffs, a route that dates back to prehistoric times, as evidenced by petroglyphs and other artifacts scattered along the way. In the 1870s, Mormon pioneers had upgraded this trail into a wagon road so that colonists from Utah could settle the valley of the Little Colorado River. Later, single men and women would return to Utah, usually to St. George, to be married in the Mormon temple, and then enjoy their honeymoon on the trip back to Arizona. Thus, the route became known as the Honeymoon Trail.

The Echo Cliffs eventually angle toward the Colorado River and force trav-

Echo Cliffs

elers to seek a crossing. Hall and Doyle descended a dugway, which "looked as if it had been cut out of the red clay mountains with a pocket knife; sometimes it hung out over the river so we seemed sliding into the muddy current and again the cliffs above hung over till one grew dizzy to look." At the river bank was a board with a penciled directive: "Fire a gun here if you want to cross." A little gasoline-powered boat ferried them across, and as Hall jumped out onto shore, she beamed, "my Promised Land—in the 'Arizona Strip' at last."

Upon her return, Hall wrote a series of articles extolling the importance of Arizona retaining the Strip. The next year (1912), when the territory became a state, the Strip was included.

As it was in the past, it continues to be. This is a big country with long vistas from the highway that can be deceptive. There is little indication of the deep canyons, dense woodlands, and jagged lava flows that are hidden beyond the pavement. Look across the plain and imagine ancient hunters stalking megafauna left over from the last ice age. Picture early people painting strange but wonderful images under overhangs and leaving animal figurines made of woven split twigs in high, nearly inaccessible caves. Envision three of John Wesley Powell's men climbing out of the Grand Canyon, then disappearing. It's a land made for legends…for imagination…for exploration and discovery.

Sharlot Hall

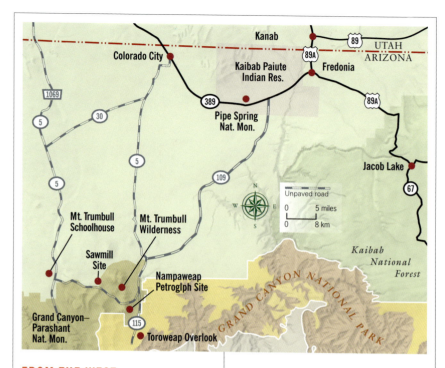

FROM THE WEST:
COLORADO CITY TO FREDONIA

Grand Canyon-Parashant National Monument

In 2000, President Bill Clinton signed a proclamation setting aside more than one million acres of the southwestern portion of the Arizona Strip as the Grand Canyon–Parashant National Monument. This monument encompasses several designated wilderness areas, part of Lake Mead National Recreation Area, and vast acreage of additional wilderness and important wildlife habitat on the Uinkaret and Shivwits Plateaus, along with the Grand Wash Cliffs.

The Uinkaret Plateau is punctuated by a series of high volcanoes: Mounts Trumbull, Emma, Logan, and Petty Knoll. In between are more than a hundred smaller cinder cones and basaltic lava flows. Its east flank is delineated by Toroweap Valley, and its west side drops off along a major fault that created the Hurricane Cliffs. Powell recorded that the Southern Paiute called this plateau Uinkaret, meaning "ponderosa pine trees sitting" or "place of the pines." A few of the Strip's off-the-pavement highlights are listed below. *Contact the Dixie/Arizona Strip Interpretive Association for more information.*

Mount Trumbull Wilderness

Mount Trumbull, the highest peak in the Uinkaret Mountains at 8,000 feet (2,441 m), is a shield volcano, meaning that it resembles a shield in profile. This type of volcano is formed by successive layers of basalt building up a mountain with moderately angled sloping sides. The mountain was named by John Wesley Powell in 1870 in honor of Illinois Senator Lyman Trumbull, who helped Powell obtain funds for his first Colorado River expedition. Nearby Mount Emma is named after Trumbull's wife.

A hiking trail climbs more than 1,500 feet (457 m) toward the summit in about 2.5 miles (4 km), but route-finding can be problematic. *Contact the Dixie/Arizona Strip Interpretive Association for more information.*

Sawmill Site and Temple Trail

Between the early 1870s and the 1940s, numerous owners and managers operated a series of sawmills on the Arizona Strip. The first one was here at the base of Mount Trumbull and provided timber and lumber for the construction of the St. George Temple, which was dedicated in 1877. The wood was hauled in wagons pulled by oxen some eighty miles to St. George over a rough road now known as the Temple Trail.

Sawmill at the base of Mount Trumbull.

Adjacent to the sawmill site (but not very apparent) is the Uinkaret Pueblo, a prehistoric Ancestral Puebloan site,

now marked by just a few lines of basalt boulders. Unfortunately, the site has been vandalized. Please do not disturb it further.

Petroglyphs carved into the basalt cliffs and boulders of Nampaweap Canyon.

Nampaweap Rock Art Site

This site is accessed by way of Mount Trumbull Road, 3 miles (4.8 km) east of the Mt. Trumbull trailhead and 3.5 miles (5.6 km) west of the Toroweap/Tuweep Road. Drive south 1.1 miles (1.8 km) on BLM Route 1028 and then turn east to the parking lot on your right. Park here and walk 0.75 mile (1.2 km) down the trail to the head of Nampaweap Canyon.

Nampaweap, derived from the Paiute words *nampaya uip*, meaning "foot canyon," contains hundreds of petroglyphs carved into the basalt cliffs and boulders in this small canyon. The rock art dates from Archaic to Paiute times. This drainage was probably an important prehistoric route between the Grand Canyon and the resources of the ponderosa pine forest around Mount Trumbull. The

Poverty Mountain   Grassy Mountain   Mt. Dellenbaugh   Surprise Canyon West Fork

predominance of bighorn sheep glyphs led local cowboys to call the place Billy Goat Canyon.

Mount Logan Wilderness

One approach is to follow the driving directions for the Nampaweap Rock Art Site but instead of parking, continue southwesterly on BLM Route 1028. The road becomes progressively worse as it approaches the wilderness boundary.

Mount Logan includes basalt ledges; cinder cones; ponderosa pine forests; piñon-juniper woodlands; and a large, colorful, naturally eroded amphitheater known as Hells Hole. The area provides habitat for deer, turkey, and Kaibab squirrels. Powell named Mount Logan for General John Logan, a senator from Illinois and a Civil War general. *Contact the Dixie/Arizona Strip Interpretive Association for more information.*

Mount Trumbull Schoolhouse

To reach the schoolhouse and former town site, take Quail Hill Road (BLM Road 1069) to Main Street Valley Road (County Road 5). Go prepared. There are no facilities.

Homesteaders began to settle this remote part of the Arizona Strip around 1916. One homesteader, Abraham Bundy, arrived after being forced out of Mexico by Pancho Villa. His family named their tiny community Mount Trumbull after the nearby volcano, but most locals called it Bundyville. By the 1930s, there were about 250 people living in the area. They dry-farmed corn, beans, wheat, squash, and other crops for their own consumption and to sell in distant towns, such as St. George, Utah. But making a living here was tough. Place names like Poverty Mountain, Hungry Valley, Last Chance Spring, and Death Valley attest to the difficult lives

Mount Trumbull schoolhouse after restoration, 1967.

Mt. Emma

Shivwits Plateau

Suicide Point

Twin Point

these pioneers led.

It is roughly sixty miles to St. George, and until the 1920s, the trip was made by horse and wagon. Drought during the 1930s made farming more difficult, so most residents turned to raising sheep or cattle. Although a few hardy souls continue to live in the area, by the 1960s, most had moved away from Mount Trumbull into the towns of Washington County, Utah, and Fredonia, Arizona.

The old Mount Trumbull schoolhouse, built in 1918, had many functions besides "learnin' the three Rs." It also served as a church, dance hall, and town meeting-house. People came from miles around to attend dances, which were the main source of entertainment. The local population declined and the school was closed in 1966.

Lumber for the school came from the pine forest to the east and was dragged by horse-drawn wagons down the Old Slide Road, so-called because it was so steep that the wagon wheels had to be locked and the wagon skidded down the incline. In 2000, vandals torched the historic building, but descendants of the first families, in cooperation with the BLM, built a replica.

Shivwits Plateau

The westernmost of the six Arizona Strip plateaus is the Shivwits, bounded on the east by the Hurricane Cliffs and on the west by the giant steps of the Grand Wash Cliffs. Only a few small mountains—Poverty Knoll, Poverty Mountain, Grassy Mountain, and Mount Dellenbaugh—relieve the relatively flat topography of the Shivwits. Frederick Dellenbaugh, who, at seventeen, had been the youngest member of Powell's second Colorado River expedition in 1871, unabashedly boasted that the mountain Powell named for him was one of the finest in the Southwest. In reality, it is only a modest volcanic cinder cone.

A mystery persists as to what became of the three men who abandoned Powell's 1869 exploratory river trip. William Dunn and Oramel and Seneca Howland left the river to climb out of the Grand Canyon to the north, toward the

Mormon settlements. Amazingly, the side canyon that they traveled up, now called Separation, was one of the few that offered passage to the rim of the Shivwits Plateau. Presumably, they made it at least as far as Mount Dellenbaugh, where a boulder on its upper slopes has Dunn's inscription plus the word "water" and an arrow pointing north.

Not long after the successful completion of Powell's river journey, the *Deseret Evening News* reported that the three men had been killed by Indians. Once Powell was back East, he received a telegraph message relaying this information. The following year, 1870, Powell spent six days exploring the Strip with the help of Mormon scout Jacob Hamblin in hopes of learning more about the men's disappearance. Powell and Hamblin encountered a band of Shivwits Paiutes, and with Hamblin translating, the Indians supposedly confessed to killing the three white men. The Indians claimed that they had mistaken them for several drunken prospectors who had killed a woman from a neighboring tribe. And that became the official historical record.

But then in the 1980s, rumors began to circulate that the Indians were not the culprits. Instead, Powell's three men had encountered some Mormons, who believed they were federal government spies. At this time, Mormon suspicion was rampant and emotions ran high, especially in southern Utah, because of the U.S. government's intervention in Utah Territory's affairs following the massacre of immigrant families at Mountain Meadows in 1857.

This historical revision purports that the three were taken to the tiny hamlet of Toquerville, Utah, near today's Zion National Park. For some unknown reason, they were killed, and the people involved swore themselves to secrecy. Although this story has spread among river guides and others as gospel, recent research casts doubt on its veracity. Three people (not related to Powell's men) did tragically meet their demise in southwestern Utah in 1869, an incident well-documented in contemporary newspapers. (If you are curious, see historian Don Lago's book *The Powell Expedition: New Discoveries about John Wesley Powell's 1869 River Journey*.)

In the remote Surprise Canyon that cuts into the Shivwits Plateau, biologists have discovered what may turn out to be a new species of leopard frog, tentatively named *Lithobates (Rana) onca*. Leopard frogs of various species once occurred in a number of springs, streams, and riparian zones on the Colorado Plateau, but are now scarce or gone from former habitats. The reasons are unclear, but it's likely that a combination of habitat loss, changing climate, and predation by introduced predators (such as trout) is to blame.

Kaibab Paiute Reservation

Neung'we Tuvip is the traditional homeland of the Kaibab Paiute, one of seven bands of Southern Paiute. The homeland stretches from Grand Canyon on the south to the northeast drainages of the Virgin River on the north, and from Kanab Canyon on the west to the

Petroglyphs often include images of bighorn sheep.

Paria River on the east. Their territory ranges in elevation from about 2,000 feet (610 m) at the Colorado River to over 9,000 feet (2,743 m) on the Kaibab Plateau, thus incorporating a wide range of natural habitats containing a variety of resources needed for survival. Their many sacred sites across the Arizona Strip and within the Grand Canyon are monitored by tribal members.

According to Kaibab Paiute, their ancestors were the E'nengweng. This is the prehistoric culture that archaeologists have termed Anasazi, or more recently, Ancestral Puebloan. Archaeologists generally believe that the earlier people left before the Kaibab Paiute ancestors arrived about AD 1100. The Kaibab Paiutes believe that the scattered panels of ancient *tumpee'po'ohp* (pictographs and petroglyphs) are sacred links to their ancestors.

Traditionally, the Paiutes moved through their territory seasonally to take advantage of ripening fruits and seeds and to hunt deer, bighorn sheep, and other animals. They built conical brush and branch shelters called *kahn* for sleeping and protection from inclement weather. As the dominant culture of the twentieth century encroached upon them, traditional living became increasingly difficult. Tragically, by 1873, the majority of the Kaibab Band was dead from disease, war, and starvation.

Paiutes depended heavily on gathering grass seeds to grind into meal; however, overgrazing by pioneer livestock had essentially denuded the grasslands by the 1880s.Their neighboring relatives, the Shivwits and Uinkaret Bands, were forced off the Arizona Strip in 1891 to reservations in southwest Utah.

The Kaibab Paiutes were granted a reservation of their own in 1907. Some became cattle ranchers and others worked for white settlers. Local ranchers continued to use much of the reservation land until a federal lawsuit removed them in 1925.

From 1994 to 1996, the Kaibab Paiutes ran a small gambling casino, but its proximity to Las Vegas kept it from being very profitable. Today, the tribe operates a convenience store and gas station, along with an RV park and campground. Some tribal members work at Pipe Spring National Monument, which is located within the reservation. Although not an easy task, they are dedicated to preserving their culture and language.

Pipe Spring National Monument

On the vast, thirsty Arizona Strip, free-flowing Pipe Spring at the base of the Vermilion Cliffs has been a welcome oasis for thousands of years. (Recently, minor earthquakes have reduced its

Winsor Castle at Pipe Spring National Monument.

flow.) First, nomadic hunter-gatherers depended upon its water; they were followed by Ancestral Puebloan farmers and, later, by the Kaibab Paiutes. Probably the first non-Indian to visit the spring was Antonio Armijo in the winter of 1829. With a pack train of mules, Armijo and his men were making their way from New Mexico to California along what would become known as the Old Spanish Trail (this trail has a number of variations).

About twenty years later, when the Mormon Church called its members to spread out from the Salt Lake Valley to found settlements in other parts of the Intermountain West, a few ranchers were drawn to the Strip's desert grasslands. In 1863, Dr. James Whitmore, a Mormon convert and cattleman from Texas, moved sheep and cattle to the Pipe Spring area. Whitmore and his herder, Robert McIntyre, built a dugout and corrals and planted an orchard and vineyard. Three years later, Navajos who had escaped capture by Kit Carson and the U.S. Army crossed the Colorado River to steal stock and ended up killing both men. Navajo raids continued on the southern Utah-northern Arizona frontier. In 1868, the Utah Militia built a small rock house (now part of the East Cabin) at the spring, from which they made one or two forays to keep the marauders southeast of the Colorado River.

Although leaders of the Navajo tribe had signed a peace treaty with the United States in 1868, they did not consider Mormons to be U.S. citizens. Peace between Navajos and Mormons finally came two years later, when Jacob Hamblin and John Wesley Powell held a peace talk between the Indians and the settlers.

Brigham Young purchased the ranch for the Mormon Church from Whitmore's widow. Young then called upon Anson Perry Winsor to manage it as a tithing ranch for the church. To safeguard Winsor and his family, two sandstone buildings facing a courtyard were constructed. Gates at each end of the courtyard enclosed both the space and the main spring. A relay station for the Deseret Telegraph system was installed, connecting this remote outpost with other Mormon settlements, including Salt Lake City. Winsor Castle, as it became known, never experienced an attack.

Church ownership lasted until 1895. Then, after passing through the hands of several owners, the "castle" fell into disrepair. In 1923, Pipe Spring was designated a national monument by President Warren Harding and restored. Today, the monument offers visitors a glimpse of American Indian and western pioneer

*At 3,000 vertical feet (915 m) above the Colorado River,
Toroweap Overlook offers a dramatic view.*

history. The Pipe Spring National Monument-Kaibab Band of Paiutes Visitor Center and Museum, operated jointly by the National Park Service and the Paiute Tribe, provides an opportunity to learn about the history and modern culture of the Kaibab Paiutes, their interactions with other tribes and cultures, and the movement of Mormon settlers into the area. Winsor Castle is fully restored and tours are conducted daily. Summer programs include ranger talks and rangers in period dress demonstrating pioneer and Indian lifeways.

Toroweap Overlook

For those well-equipped visitors who are looking for an adventure, a trip out to Toroweap Overlook fits the bill. However,

it's 60 rough miles south of Pipe Spring, at the end of Toroweap (AKA Tuweep) Valley. Toroweap Overlook, an icon of western Grand Canyon, is frequented by landscape photographers and geologists but seldom visited by the average tourist. There are no services, and cell phone coverage is spotty at best. The park service campground requires an advance reservation. Allow at least two or three hours each way to traverse the bone-jarring dirt road; flat tires are not uncommon. A high-clearance vehicle is recommended. (A visit to nps.gov/grca/planyourvisit/tuweep.htm for the latest information on road conditions and camping regulations is highly recommended.)

One translation of Toroweap is "deep

gorge." Here, the canyon is quite narrow and drops approximately 3,000 vertical feet (900 m) to the Colorado River. Downstream, you can see and hear Lava Falls. Though it looks like a riffle from the rim, it is one of the most treacherous of the Colorado's rapids.

Vulcans Throne and lava cascades.

When explorer John Wesley Powell encountered Lava Falls, he exclaimed, "What a conflict of water and fire there must have been here! Just imagine a river of molten rock running down into a river of melted snow. What a seething and boiling of the waters; what clouds of steam rolled into the heavens!"

Although Vulcans Throne, a cinder cone, sits prominently on the canyon rim above the rapids, the black lava cascading down the canyon wall came from cones farther north on the western edge of Toroweap Valley. Beginning approximately 630,000 years ago, these flows created lava dams across the Colorado River, which backed up into huge lakes. The lakes eventually filled, overflowing the dams and eroding the lava. Remnants of these dams (one of which was more than 2,000 feet/610 m high) are visible as horizontal layers of basalt at the base of the cascades. However, the modern-day rapids here are not remnants of one of these igneous dams. Rather, debris flows and flash floods have washed boulders and sediment out of Prospect Canyon, constricting the river and forming the rapids. Debris flows are made up of a slurry of sediment and water that typically contains more than 80 percent solids. These sediments can range from clay particles to extraordinarily huge boulders; in a 1990 debris flow, one of these boulders weighed an estimated 290 tons (263,000 kg).

In 1995, members of a research trip were camped near the mouth of Prospect Canyon, where they were studying past debris flows, when a tremendous rainstorm hit during the night. They were startled to hear a roaring sound that they interpreted as being the Colorado River rising from storm runoff. They feared that their camp and boats were being threatened, but after a few minutes, the noise subsided. In the morning, they discovered a new debris fan coming out of Prospect Canyon, which was constricting part of the Colorado River at Lava Falls Rapid, creating monstrous waves and trapping them above an unrunnable rapid. However, as they watched, the river promptly began to erode the edge of the debris fan, and by afternoon, a navigable passage through Lava Falls developed.

The scientists later determined that this 1995 debris flow was the third largest to occur at this location in 100 years—an astonishing thing to have witnessed.

One person comes to mind when speaking of Toroweap country: Ranger John Riffey. Riffey was one of those rare, remarkable individuals who relished remote places as much as any hermit but was also affable and friendly to a fault. Unlike many NPS rangers, who transfer from park to park throughout their careers, Riffey steadfastly manned his post in Toroweap Valley for nearly forty years.

When he was first assigned to this

Ranger John Riffey

lonely outpost in Grand Canyon National Monument in 1942, his job was to make sure that overgrazing did not occur within the monument, where some pre-existing grazing leases had been "grandfathered" in when the monument was established. In the early days, it was an all-day drive to Kanab, the nearest town. But Riffey learned to fly his own airplane, a Super Cub, which he christened Pogo. He also nicknamed most of the park service equipment. George was the barometer; Matilda was the front-end loader; Sparky, of course, was the generator; and Big Scratchy was the road grader.

Whether it was while getting directions to Lava Falls Trail or as they munched on homemade chocolate-chip cookies, all who met Riffey and his second wife, fervent ornithologist Meribeth, remember their kindness and good cheer. They're both gone now, but they are laid to rest not far from their beloved Grand Canyon home.

This isolated part of the park was established as Grand Canyon National Monument by President Herbert Hoover in 1932. In spite of its inaccessibility, annual visitation at Toroweap reached 1,000 by the 1960s, and it was officially added to the park as part of the Grand Canyon Enlargement Act in 1975.

Kanab Creek Wilderness

Another spectacular area to explore is the Kanab Creek Wilderness, adjacent to the national park. Kanab Creek flows to the Colorado River and has carved a splendid canyon. Several trails suitable for hikers or pack animals lead into it.

Kanab Canyon has been called the "route of scientists." Geologists J. W. Powell (1872), G. K. Gilbert (1872), and Charles Walcott (1879) all passed through it. Powell ended his second descent of the Colorado River at the mouth of Kanab Creek. He had employed George Riley and John Bonnemort to assist in his surveys. While they waited at the mouth of Kanab Creek, they panned the sands along the Colorado and found a little extremely fine gold, called flour gold. Word of the discovery spread like wildfire, and before long, hundreds of hopeful prospectors began pouring down Kanab Creek. The rush lasted four months before the fortune-seekers real-

Kanab Creek Wilderness Trail, Snake Gulch.

ized that the flour gold was too dispersed to be economically mined.

The main side canyon used to access Kanab was Snake Gulch, which contains world-class prehistoric rock art. The pictographs and petroglyphs range in age from Archaic to historic Paiute. Latter-day explorers, prospectors, cowboys, and early tourists also left inscriptions.

In 1872, geologist Grove Karl Gilbert, a member of the U.S. Army–regulated Wheeler expedition, visited the North Rim and descended Kanab Creek to the river in 1872. Along the way, he encountered members of the Powell party, including the major's cousin, Clement. Gilbert later met John Wesley Powell in Salt Lake City and by 1875, had accepted Powell's invitation to join his independent survey.

From mid-August until mid-November 1879, Charles D. Walcott was assigned the task of "measuring section" in the Grand Canyon region. This meant identifying and measuring the thickness of each sedimentary rock formation to define geologic columns. He started with the youngest, uppermost beds exposed near Bryce Canyon and traveled down Kanab Creek to the river. In that eighty-mile lateral distance with a hand level, chain, and altimeter, he and his crew measured 13,000 feet of vertical section. Age measurements in the next century would show that he had covered 500 million years of Earth's history, from the Eocene to the Cambrian. It might be the longest continuous geologic section ever measured, there being few other places in the world where 2.5 miles of vertically exposed sedimentary rock are accessible in one eighty-mile stretch.

Copper was discovered in breccia pipe deposits (irregular cylindrical masses of fragmented rock that accumulate minerals from ground water) about 1890 in Hacks Canyon, another of Kanab's side canyons. However, it wasn't until 1945 that miners realized that uranium oxide was also present. The uranium boom of the 1950s spurred further interest in these deposits, and tons of copper and uranium ore were shipped to Salt Lake City for processing. Low concentrations limited profit, and the property changed hands many times before being idled in 1964. A second uranium boom in the 1970s (and increased prices for the ore) led another owner, Energy Fuels Nuclear, to reopen the mines and undertake exploratory drilling for other deposits. The mines were active until 1988, when it was assumed that the ore was depleted; plus, the price of uranium was falling. It was one of the few profitable mining ventures in the Grand Canyon region, largely due to faster, more efficient modern equipment.

decided that while their husbands were off working, they would torch the saloon.

By chance, the saloonkeeper saw the angry wives coming, so he rolled the building across the state line into Arizona. As the women readied their torches, he admonished them, "You can't touch this business; it's in Arizona." At that point, the women went home in disgust.

Later, wives in Fredonia also got fed up with their husbands' drinking and came riding down on the saloon. Again, the saloonkeeper saw them coming and pushed the bar into Utah. This back-and-forth rolling of the saloon went on for years—according to the old cowboy, at least.

Rowland Rider was a full-time wrangler on the Strip from 1907 until 1910, then cowboyed for a number of years during the summer. In 1919, he served as marshal of Kanab before moving to Salt Lake City in 1928. He was fortunate to cross paths with many of the

FROM THE NORTH: KANAB TO ENTRANCE STATION

From Kanab, Utah, a short 7-mile (11.3-km) drive south on U.S. Highway 89A brings you to Fredonia. Halfway in between is the Arizona-Utah border on the 37th Parallel, the exact location of which was fixed by the Powell Survey during their 1871–1872 winter season.

According to an old cowboy by the name of Rowland Rider, it was here on the border that a little saloon was constructed back in the 1890s. A two-room affair, it had a bar at one end and the barkeeper's bedroom at the other. The entire building sat on top of log rollers. Not surprisingly, this establishment was very popular with the local cowboys. However, their wives were none too happy. One day, the women in Kanab

Rowland Rider at a rodeo in Kanab, 1912.

historically interesting characters that traveled through that country in the early twentieth century, including Zane Grey, Butch Cassidy, and President Theodore Roosevelt. Later in life, Rider's infectious laugh, love of nature, and continuing sense of wonderment, coupled with an absolute memory for detail, made him a popular storyteller. Many of his delightful tales (true or not) have been preserved in the book *The Roll Away Saloon: Cowboy Tales of the Arizona Strip*, written by Rider's granddaughter, Deirdre Paulsen.

Fredonia began to be settled in about 1885 as a ranching outpost of Kanab. Many names were suggested for the growing community—Hardscrabble, Lickskillet, Freedonkey, and Rockford—before residents eventually decided on Stewart. Later, it was changed to Union for a few years, then back to Stewart. In 1889, residents finally settled on Fredonia, which had been suggested by Apostle Erastus Snow as representative of families seeking freedom from federal polygamy laws, and it has been that ever since. (Some of the locals view the "donia" part of the name as a corruption of the Spanish word for wife—*doña*—thus the additional implication of those with extra wives having a place to escape the law.)

North Kaibab Ranger District

As you continue south of Fredonia, the highway climbs from sagebrush desert through piñon-juniper woodland into ponderosa pine forest. Most of the Kaibab Plateau's land was set aside as the Grand Canyon Forest Reserve by President Benjamin Harrison in 1893, and renamed the Kaibab National Forest in 1908. This act did not preclude grazing, mining, or lumbering. Then in 1906, President Theodore Roosevelt created the Grand Canyon Game Preserve, which included more than 612,000 acres (247,676 hectares) of the Kaibab National Forest, to be "set aside for the protection of game animals and birds." In 1965, 200,000 acres of Kaibab National Forest was designated as the Kaibab Squirrel Area, a national natural landmark, specifically to protect the habitat of this endemic squirrel. Today, this land is managed by the North Kaibab Ranger District of the U.S. Forest Service.

Lefevre Overlook

Along the highway is the Lefevre Overlook, named after an early local ranching family. This is a good place to stop and take in the panoramic view to the north toward Utah. On a clear day, you can see from Glen Canyon National Recreation Area to the east over to Zion National Park on the west and north to the Beaver Mountains.

To the north, a series of ascending cliffs rise like a staircase, much of which is included in the Grand Staircase-Escalante National Monument. Each step represents millions of years of geologic time. Underfoot is Kaibab Limestone, the same layer that makes up the rim of the Grand Canyon. The limestone slopes gently downward to the north and underlies all that you see.

Looking beyond the piñon-juniper woodland below, you'll see the risers

The Grand Staircase panoramic view at Lefevre Overlook.

of the "staircase," known locally as the Chocolate Cliffs (Moenkopi Formation), Vermilion Cliffs (Moenave Formation), White Cliffs (Navajo Sandstone), Gray Cliffs (various Cretaceous formations), and Pink Cliffs (Claron Formation). The Moenkopi Formation is about 230 million years old and the top Claron Formation is roughly 45 million, a perfect example of the "layer cake" makeup of the Colorado Plateau's geology: younger rocks atop older rocks.

There may be Navajo craftspeople selling their wares at this overlook. These venders work under a permit system authorized by the North Kaibab Ranger District.

From Leferve Overlook, the highway continues to gain elevation and the woodland gives way to ponderosa pine forest.

Jacob Lake Inn

In 1923, Harold and Nina Bowman, descendants of local pioneers, established a gas station along the old Grand Canyon Highway next to Jacob Lake, where "Fill'er up!" meant siphoning gasoline out of fifty-gallon barrels. Within a year, they had built a small two-room cabin on a ridge overlooking the lake. In 1929, a new road bypassed the lake, so the Bowmans relocated to the present site at the junction of U.S. Highway 89A and Arizona Highway 67. During the winter months, Jacob Lake Inn serves as jumping-off point for snowmobilers, cross-country skiers, and snowshoers. Highway 67 is closed to vehicles until the snow melts, which is usually around mid-May.

Next to the inn is the Kaibab Plateau Visitor Center, operated by the U.S. Forest Service and the Grand Canyon Conservancy. This is a great place to acquire information, maps, books, and

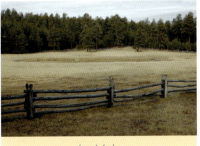

Jacob Lake

other material about the area.

About 0.5-mile (0.8 km) south of the Jacob Lake Inn, turn west onto Forest Road 461 and drive 0.75 mile (1.2 km) to Jacob Lake, which is really just a pond even in wet years. It was named after the Mormon scout Jacob Hamblin. Here, you'll also find the original Jacob Lake Ranger Station, built in 1910, just five years after the U.S. Forest Service was established. The cabin and barn, among the oldest surviving forest service administrative buildings, were restored in 2015–2016.

Restored ranger station at Jacob Lake.

At the cabin, a pedestal made of blue and green mineralized rocks supports an interpretive sign. These rocks are azurite and malachite, copper carbonate ores, from nearby small deposits that were mined from the mid- to late-1880s. The ore was transported to Ryan (now abandoned), about seven miles west, to be smelted.

The Scenic Byway: Arizona Highway 67

Providing the road is open, any time is a lovely time to drive Arizona Highway 67, a 31-mile (50-km) scenic byway, from Jacob Lake Inn to the Grand Canyon National Park entrance station. Autumn is an especially colorful season, when aspen leaves have turned brilliant gold and the tree-tops flame with color. In the lower, wetter areas of the meadows, clover, mountain dandelion, wild daisies, sedges, and buttercups bloom. On their drier perimeters, buckwheat, pussytoes, cinquefoil, saxifrage, phlox, mountain parsley, and grasses are common. Purple lupine and red penstemon grace the road's shoulders, and a few New Mexican locusts still sport pink blooms. The flowering season comes late at this elevation (8,000 feet/2,450 m).

But don't hurry. Stop often as possible at any of the scenic turnouts. Listen for the eerie, liquid, flutelike phrases sung by a hidden hermit thrush; look for a cautious bobcat creeping down to a sinkhole for a drink; admire the mule deer browsing or bison grazing at the edge of DeMotte Park; laugh at the antics of a rafter of wild turkeys stopping traffic as they gobble their way across the road; and be alert for the flash of a snowy white tail on the south end of a

Wild turkeys

northbound Kaibab Squirrel or the sudden flush of the rare blue grouse.

Beginning about six miles from Jacob Lake, you enter an area that has obviously been burned. On June 8, 2006, lightning ignited a fire about fourteen miles north of the Grand Canyon National Park boundary. For a week and a half, the Warm Fire burned at a low level of intensity, and the U.S. Forest Service considered it useful—it would clean the forest floor of accumulated pine duff, leaves, and dead branches. Also, burning some small trees and shrubs would help open up the forest. Low-intensity fires return nutrients to the soil and increase the growth of perennial grasses, forbs, and browse plants that, in turn, enhance wildlife habitat. They also reduce the potential for high-intensity fires that can destroy wildlife habitat.

On June 18, high winds from the southwest began to push the fire northeastward, and suppression tactics were initiated, in part to protect buildings and structures at Jacob Lake. However, the fire's intensity dramatically increased during the evening of June 25. Fortunately, weather conditions began to change the next day; scattered rain showers fell on the 27th, but it took more than a week to contain the fire completely. By then, 58,630 acres (23,728 hectares) had burned.

Some of the highest-intensity burning occurred along Arizona Highway

Phlox

67, turning once-lovely forest and meadow into devastated landscapes of gray and black ash. However, about 65 percent (38,360 acres/15,524 hectares) of the area burned at low intensity, and rains later that summer began to heal the forest. Wildlife, such as deer, quickly moved back into the burned area.

DeMotte Park

About 23 miles (37 km) from Jacob Lake, the road enters 8-mile-long DeMotte Park. While preparing for his second descent of the Colorado River through the Grand Canyon in 1872, Powell traveled from Kanab, Utah, to Big Spring and on to the North Rim. He was

Demotte Park meadow

accompanied by Professor Almon Harris Thompson and his wife, Nellie; George Adair; two Indian guides; and Harvey C. DeMotte. While passing through this lovely meadow, Powell decided to name it after his friend DeMotte, a professor of mathematics at Wesleyan University in Illinois. The meadow is also called V.T. Park by local cattlemen ("park" being a cowboy term for meadow and VT being a historic local brand).

RAINBOW RIM TRAIL

Accessed by various dirt and gravel forest service roads from DeMotte Park, this trail is becoming popular with mountain bikers as well as hikers. It's a more than 20-mile (32-km) drive to its several trailheads, and going can be slow and rough. But the trail winds along the canyon rim with intimate views into Crazy Jug and Saddle Canyons and expansive views of the Grand Canyon to the west and southwest.

Near the south end of DeMotte Park, forest service roads veer off west and east, leading to the Rainbow Rim Trail and East Rim Viewpoint, respectively, both of which are outside the park.

East Rim Viewpoint

A 2.5-mile (4 km) graded road leads east from Arizona Highway 67 to the East Rim Viewpoint, which offers exquisite views. The broad Marble Platform spreads out before you, bordered on the north and east by the Vermilion and Echo Cliffs, respectively. Lees Ferry is

at the place where the two sets of cliffs almost come together. The huge gorge incised into the relatively flat Marble Platform is Marble Canyon, the upper reaches of the Grand Canyon. Due east, squatting between Echo Cliffs and Marble Canyon, is the low, flat-topped mesa known as Shinumo Altar. While mapping the Kaibab in 1872, Frederick Dellenbaugh spied the mesa. He noted, "It stood up so like a great altar and, having in mind the house-building Amerinds who had formerly occupied the country, and whom the Pai Utes [sic] called Shinumo. I called it Shinumo Altar, the name it now bears. ...It was the appearance that suggested the title, not any archaeological find."

Several trails cross at the East Rim Viewpoint. Running parallel to the eastern edge of the Kaibab Plateau is the Arizona Trail (this segment is sometimes called the Kaibab Plateau Trail). The Arizona Trail starts at the Arizona-Utah border, goes south to meet the North Kaibab Trail, and offers a non-motorized corridor for the entire length of Arizona south to the Mexican border.

Descending the East Kaibab Monocline into the valley below is the North Canyon Trail. It's about 7 miles (11.3 km) in length and drops nearly 3,000 vertical feet (914 m) on its way through the Saddle Mountain Wilderness Area to House Rock Valley. The trail goes down through mixed conifer and oak thickets into North Canyon, passing stands of old-growth aspen. It continues back and forth across a small perennial stream that supports a lush riparian habitat, into

Vermilion Cliffs   Navajo Mountain   Echo Cliffs   Shinumo Altar

East Rim Viewpoint offers a splendid view of the Marble Platform and the canyon's northernmost section.

which endangered Apache trout have been introduced. (Originally, Apache trout were only found in the White Mountains of east-central Arizona.)

The next tributary canyon downstream from North is, appropriately, South Canyon. A rough scrambling route exists down South Canyon to the river, a way not recommended for novice Grand Canyon hikers. Near the mouth of South Canyon is the large opening to Stantons Cave, and several hundred yards down-river bursts forth Vaseys Paradise, a lovely perennial spring that cascades from several openings in the Redwall Limestone. Vaseys Paradise is named for physician-turned-botanist George W. Vasey, who accompanied Powell on his 1868 Rocky Mountain Scientific Exploring Expedition.

Stantons Cave is named for Robert Brewster Stanton, an intrepid engineer who in 1889–1890 surveyed a water-level railroad route through the Grand Canyon. In July 1889, after three men in Stanton's expedition drowned, he and the four remaining men cached their boats and supplies in the cave and hiked out. Within six months, he returned, this time with life jackets, and completed the survey.

The more than 100 split-willow twig figurines of deer or bighorn sheep found in the cave have been attributed to members of the Archaic Pinto Basin Culture, who lived in the canyon region about 4,000 years ago. The figurines may have been some sort of hunting magic. A number of animal bones have been recovered from the cave as well. Most belonged to species still living in the canyon. However, several exciting finds included bone fragments of the extinct Merriam's teratorn, a very large vulture with a 12-foot/3.6-m wingspan (by comparison, today's turkey vulture has a mere 5.5 foot/1.7 m wingspan) and Harrington mountain goat, both apparently common animals during the Ice Age.

shoots across the Marble Platform, and begins a steep climb up the wavelike crustal fold called the East Kaibab Monocline. From desert grassland dotted with rabbitbrush, big sage, broom snakeweed, and salt bush, the road ascends through piñon-juniper woodland, which is then replaced by ponderosa pine forest as the road climbs in elevation to Jacob Lake.

FROM THE EAST: MARBLE CANYON TO JACOB LAKE

To reach the North Rim from the south or east, take U.S. Highway 89 through the western section of the vast Navajo Reservation to the U.S. Highway 89A turnoff. If you happen to be coming from the Glen Canyon National Recreation Area and Page, this turnoff will be at the base of switchbacks that bring you down the Echo Cliffs to the Marble Platform.

Modern Highway 89A parallels the Echo and Vermilion Cliffs, following closely the old Mormon Emigrant Wagon Road from Utah (AKA the Arizona Road, or Honeymoon Trail), which traces even earlier Native American paths. There is little hint of the great canyon to the west until U.S. Highway 89A bridges the Colorado River at Marble Canyon, the name John Wesley Powell gave to the upper reaches of the Grand Canyon.

The highway then swings around the base of the towering Vermilion Cliffs,

Navajo Bridge Interpretive Center

Prior to 1929, the recommended auto route from the South Rim of the Grand Canyon to the North Rim was to first go south to unpaved Route 66, then west to Kingman, then northwest and cross the Colorado River at Searchlight, Nevada, then north and northeast to St. George, Utah, then east to Kanab and finally, south to Bright Angel Point. The trip of more than 600 dusty—or sometimes muddy—bone-jarring miles (965 km) ended up only 10 air-miles (16 air-km) from where it started.

Navajo Bridge Interpretive Center

The original Navajo Bridge is open for foot traffic.

In January 1929, a bridge spanning Marble Canyon was completed, and although the road was unpaved until 1938, increasing numbers of intrepid motorists began taking the shorter route around the eastern side of the Grand Canyon, following in the wagon-wheel ruts of the Mormon pioneers. This journey was "only" a third of the much longer one.

Marble Canyon contains no marble, but rather, polished limestone. When John Wesley Powell boated down the Colorado River in 1869, he wrote, "And now the scenery is on a grand scale. The walls of the canyon, 2,500 feet high, are of marble, of many beautiful colors, often polished below by the waves, and sometimes far up the sides, where showers have washed the sands over the cliffs. At one place I…walk for more than a mile on a marble platform, all polished and fretted with strange devices and embossed in a thousand fantastic patterns. Through a cleft in the wall the sun shines on this pavement and it gleams in iridescent beauty…we call it Marble Canyon."

When crossing Marble Canyon on the U.S. Highway 89A bridge, notice that there is a second bridge to the north (upstream). This is the original 1929 Navajo Bridge. On the east side is the Navajo Nation, and a pullout where you may find locals selling arts and crafts. On the west side is a parking area for the Navajo Bridge Interpretive Center, which is operated by the Glen Canyon Natural History Association. This is a great place to get information, maps, books, and other material about the area. Between the west end of the historic bridge and the interpretive center is a rock structure built by the Civilian Conservation Corps

The new Navajo Bridge was completed in May 1995.

during the Great Depression as a "road stop."

Take a few minutes to walk out on the old bridge for a view of the Colorado River far below. You may see boaters floating down the river, or a California condor perched on a bridge girder. This is also a good place to think about what has happened to the Colorado River over the last fifty years or so. About twenty river-miles upstream is Glen Canyon Dam. Since its completion in 1963, the Colorado River below the dam has changed dramatically. Instead of a red desert torrent "too thick to drink yet too thin to plow," it is now a clear (except during heavy storm runoff), cold waterway whose depth fluctuates according to the whims and wishes of power and irrigation companies. Before the dam, the wild Colorado River was always muddy and sometimes raging. What you see today is a tamed, regulated river.

Eight native fish species, six of which are endemic to the Colorado River system, have suffered from the changed riverine conditions. Three species are now gone from the Grand Canyon section of the river, and the remaining five are endangered. The natives laid eggs that required warm water for hatching. Now, water released from the depths of Lake Powell runs cold. Non-native fish, brown and rainbow trout, have been introduced, and these voracious predators feed upon any hatchlings that might come along.

Although trout-stocking began in a few

Rainbow trout, a non-native fish of the Colorado River.

of the canyon's clear, cool side creeks as early as 1919, the planted fish could not move out into the warm, muddy Colorado. However, after Glen Canyon Dam was completed, trout could be released directly into the river. The trout have done phenomenally well in the clear, cold water, and anglers test their skills between Lees Ferry and Glen Canyon Dam, all part of Glen Canyon National Recreation Area, which also includes Lake Powell.

Downstream, within Grand Canyon National Park (which begins at the confluence of the Paria River with the Colorado), the National Park Service is attempting to reduce the number of the non-native trout. Anglers in the park are encouraged to keep and enjoy the trout they catch.

Lees Ferry

An interesting side trip is to turn onto the spur road to Lees Ferry, just beyond the west end of Navajo Bridge. A 6-mile (8-km) scenic drive takes you to the ferry site, sometimes referred to as the crossroads of northern Arizona. Not only

Lees Ferry is the launch site for river trips through the Grand Canyon.

is Lees Ferry where river trips begin their float through the Grand Canyon, it is also a historic location. Over the years, Lees Ferry became, as writer Frank Waters called it, "Geographically our 42nd and Broadway. …For nearly four centuries everybody has eventually showed up here." It is where the Colorado River emerges from one canyon, Glen, before plunging into the next, Marble. There is about a 2-mile (3.2-km) stretch where it is relatively easy to reach the bank of the Colorado River. This ease of access doesn't occur again until 225 river miles downstream, where a gravel road on the Hualapai Reservation descends to the Colorado.

From Lees Ferry to the Kaibab Plateau, the highway closely follows the base of the towering Vermilion Cliffs. In 1984, the cliffs and Paria Canyon were designated a wilderness area; then in 2000, the wilderness plus the remote Paria Plateau became the 294,000-acre (118,982-hectare) Vermilion Cliffs National Monument. *More information and hiking permits for the spectacular Paria Canyon and the Coyote Buttes area can be obtained online at blm.gov/az/paria.*

Crossing the Colorado

In October 1776, Spanish padres Silvestre Vélez de Escalante and Francisco Atanasio Domínguez attempted to cross the Colorado here, close to where the Paria River enters the main river. "To do this, two of those who knew how to swim well entered the river naked with their clothes upon their heads. It was so deep and wide that the swimmers, in spite of their prowess, were barely able to reach the other side, leaving in midstream their clothing, which they never saw again. And since they became so exhausted getting there, nude and barefoot, they were unable to walk far enough to do said exploring, coming back across after having paused a while to catch their breath."

They seemed to be trapped. "We are surrounded on all sides by mesas and big hogbacks impossible to climb," the padres recorded in their notes. Understandably depressed, they named their camp *San Benito de Salsipuedes*, meaning, "get out if you can." However, they eventually located a route a short way up the Paria River that led over the cliffs and back down to an easier crossing further up the Colorado. (This adventuresome route is occasionally used today by hikers. Check with the Lees Ferry ranger for directions and precautions.)

Other travelers passed this way as well. In *The Last of the Plainsmen* (1908), Zane Grey wrote, "I saw the constricted rapids, where the Colorado took its plunge into the box-like head of the Grand Cañon…and the deep, reverberating boom of the river, at flood height, was a fearful thing to hear. I could not repress a shudder at the thought of crossing above that rapid."

Even crossing the unruly Colorado by ferry was exciting, and sometimes dangerous. As the Navajo Bridge was being constructed in 1928, two passengers and ferryman Adolph Johnson drowned when the ferry torqued and flipped in a whirlpool.

For another perspective, in 1911, Arizona historian Sharlot Hall gushed, "We dropped down over a lot of hills that seemed made out of all the scrapings of the Painted Desert and saw a big copper line like a badly twisted snake crawling along below with the greenest fields I ever saw beyond it and the reddish cliffs behind them. …It was as beautiful as it was wild and strange and I doubt if there is a wilder, stranger spot in the Southwest."

In August 1940, young, not-yet-Arizona-senator Barry Goldwater arrived at Lees Ferry on a Norman Nevills river trip. He remarked, "Beautiful, historic, restful—Lees Ferry always has been one of my favorite spots."

John D. Lee and Lonely Dell Ranch

It's called Lees Ferry, but who was this Lee character? In 1857, a wagon train passing through Mountain Meadows, southwest of Cedar City, Utah, was attacked by the Utah Militia and (possibly) Paiute Indians. About 120 men, women, and children were killed. Only seventeen young children were spared. The reasons and events that led up to this massacre are complex, but suffice it to say that the Mormon participants thought they were protecting their families. Others saw it as a brutal, unjustifiable act. Regardless, only one person was ever singled out for the crime: John Doyle Lee.

John Doyle Lee with two of his wives, ca. 1875.

Elders in the Church of Jesus Christ of Latter-day Saints suggested that Lee

Homestead cabin at Lonely Dell.

make himself scarce, so—wives and children in tow—he headed off into the wilds of southern Utah. He established the ferry and ranch at the head of the Grand Canyon near the mouth of the Paria River. Back in 1858, Jacob Hamblin, a Mormon scout, explorer, and missionary, had reported that there was good land there, and named the spot "Lonely Dell."

When Lee and part of his large family arrived in December 12, 1871, his seventeenth wife, Emma, agreed with Hamblin's appellation, and the name stuck. Within a month, on January 29, the ferry had its first customers when a band of fifteen Navajos called for a ride from the east side. However, the only craft available was an old flatboat, the *Cañon Maid*, which had been abandoned by Powell. Lee's sixth wife, Rachel, volunteered to steer the flimsy craft while Lee rowed.

Not until the following year, on January 11, 1873, was a proper ferry boat constructed and launched. One important reason for maintaining a ferry at this location was that Mormon Church leaders were concerned that their people might be forced to move from Utah to more tolerant Mexico, in part because of their practice of polygamy. A ferry here, they thought, would aid the exodus.

John D. Lee's ferry in mid-river, 1925.

HIKES WORTH CONSIDERING

One descends Cathedral Wash about 1.5 miles (2.4 km) to a sandy beach on the river and is popular with fishermen. The trailhead is along the Lees Ferry Road, a little over 1 mile (1.6 km) from Highway 89A.

The other is Spencer Trail, which ascends the cliffs about 0.5 mile (0.8 km) upstream from the north end of the Lees Ferry parking area. Follow the path that parallels the river. Spencer Trail begins just about opposite the wreckage of the *Charles H. Spencer*. The trail wastes no time, switch-backing 1,500 feet (457 m) in 1.5 miles (2.4 km) up the Vermilion Cliffs, rewarding the hiker with superlative views of the river and the head of Marble Canyon, the dramatic beginning of the Grand Canyon.

The trail is named after Charles H. Spencer, one of canyon country's more colorful prospectors and entrepreneurs. Gold was known to occur in small quantities in the green shales of the Chinle Formation at the base of the Vermilion Cliffs. Spencer's plan was to set up a system of hydraulic hoses to shoot Colorado River water at the shale slopes, then send the dissolved material down a long flume to an amalgamator. He built this trail in 1910 in order to use mule trains to transport coal from Warm Creek, some 28 miles (45 km) north, to Lees Ferry; the coal was to be used to power pumps and sluices. But after the trail was completed, he decided that mule trains could not carry enough coal, and so hatched another scheme.

Spencer had a dismantled 92-foot (28-m) paddle wheel steamboat hauled in by wagon and reconstructed at the mouth of Warm Creek. The boat was christened the *Charles H. Spencer*, loaded with coal, and set off to Lees Ferry. Unfortunately, Spencer discovered that much of the coal the boat could carry would be needed just to make the round trip. Additionally, tests showed that the amount of gold in the Chinle shale was too small to be profitable. The *Charles H. Spencer* was moored and eventually sank. Undaunted, Spencer continued to prospect unsuccessfully in the area for more than fifty years, seeking his fortune.

Spencer's gold processing rig at Lees Ferry, 1911

Because Lee stayed on the move to avoid capture, Emma became the driving force behind the ranching and ferry operations. Ultimately, however, Lee was caught, and after two trials (the first ended in a hung jury), was sentenced to be death by firing squad in Mountain Meadows. His grave is in Panguitch, Utah.

To visit the Lonely Dell Ranch, historic cemetery, and fruit orchard, turn off the Lees Ferry Road just before it crosses the Paria River, five miles from Highway 89A, park, and walk the short distance to the sites.

Remains of an early homestead and tourist attraction.

Cliff Dwellers

As Highway 89A skirts around the head of Soap Creek, what looks like a collection of ancient dwellings tucked next to and under oversized boulders appears. These are actually the remains of an early homestead and tourist attraction. In 1927, New Yorker Blanche Russell's car broke down near here. While awaiting rescue, she fell in love with the grandiose scenery and decided to buy a parcel.

Several years later, she and her husband Bill constructed the little stone buildings to attract tourists.

San Bartolomé Historic Turnout

About 19 miles (30.5 km) west of the Navajo Bridge (or 0.5 mile/0.8 km west of Milepost 557) is the scenic San Bartolomé Historic Turnout. In 1776, two Spanish padres, Fray Francisco Atanasio Domínguez and Fray Silvestre Vélez de Escalante, attempted to reach the Monterey Missions in California.

But they left Santa Fe, New Mexico, too late in the year; by the time they reached the Great Basin region of western Utah, winter snows were beginning to close the high mountain passes. Instead of retracing their steps, their Indian guides took them on a route that ran south toward the Grand Canyon and then east to avoid the gorge. As they crossed the Arizona Strip, they encountered the Southern Paiute people, who provided them with food and showed them the way across the Strip.

The Spaniards camped near this spot, naming it San Bartolomé on the night of October 24, 1776. As their journal entries describe, "Here there is extensive valley land but of bad terrain, for what is not sand is a kind of ground having about three inches of rubble, and after that loose soil of different hues. There are many deposits of transparent

The Echo Cliffs flank Highway 89 and parallel the Colorado River below Lees Ferry.

gypsum, some of mica, and there also seems to be some of metallic ore."

John Wesley Powell, who passed by almost a century later, wrote, "[W]e left behind a long line of cliffs, many hundred feet high, composed of orange and vermilion sandstones. I have named them 'Vermilion Cliffs.' When we are out a few miles I look back and see the morning sun shining in splendor on their painted faces; the salient angles are on fire, and the retreating angles are buried in shade, and I gaze on them until my vision dreams and the cliffs appear a long bank of purple clouds piled from the horizon high into the heavens."

As you look toward the cliffs, a major indentation marks the approximate location of natural springs variously known as Jacob's Pools or Rachel's Pools. Late in 1872, Lee was advised that he would be safer at Jacob's Pools than down by the Colorado River. So he took his sixth wife, Rachel; her family; and most of his cattle and built another ranch, which he called Doyle's Retreat. But he didn't linger here long, preferring to maintain a low profile, be somewhat elusive, and visit his other wives.

Buffalo Ranch Turnoff

About 2 miles (3.2 km) west of the San Bartolomé Historic Turnout, an unpaved road leads 22 miles (35.4 km) south to Buffalo Ranch, operated by the Arizona Game and Fish Department. The buffalo, or more correctly, bison, that used to live here have taken up residence mostly on the Kaibab Plateau, either in the national forest or in the park.

Vermilion Cliffs National Monument view

Vermilion Cliffs National Monument

In another 6 miles (9.6 km), there is a pullout and information board about Vermilion Cliffs National Monument's natural history and recreational opportunities.

House Rock Valley Overlook

Getting to the top of the Kaibab Plateau in a motorized vehicle used to be a much more difficult undertaking than it is today. Until the 1930s, the road climbing the East Kaibab Monocline was much steeper. Autos of the early twentieth century had gravity-fed gas lines; ascending a steep hill meant that gas wouldn't flow to the engine. The problem was solved by driving backwards.

House Rock Valley was named after a campsite near a spring against the Vermilion Cliffs, where a couple of large boulders lean together to form a crude shelter. At some point prior to 1871, someone using a piece of charcoal printed Rock House Hotel on one of the rocks. Several members of the second Powell expedition noted the inscription, and added the name to their map.

While gazing across the broad Marble Platform, coyotes, pronghorn antelope, and bison may come to mind, but a host of smaller creatures call these desert grasslands home. One is the northern grasshopper mouse, which has been described as "howling like a wolf and attacking like a lion." That might be a bit of an exaggeration, for the diminutive grasshopper mouse measures only 5 to 6 inches (12.7 to 15.2 cm) from nose to tail-tip. However, its behavior is quite different from most other mice.

Northern grasshopper mouse

Using their tail for balance, these mice rear up on their hind legs, point their head upward, and emit a tiny squeak, the so-called howl. These squeaks are actually ultrasonic calls that can be heard by other animals up to 200 feet (61 m) away. Then they're off searching for food—not seeds and vegetation like other mice, but invertebrates, reptiles, and even the occasional rodent up to three times their size. Cannibalism is not uncommon. The actions of these aggressive and combative mice have been likened to those of shrews.

Leaving the overlook, within 10 miles (16 km) you'll be back at Jacob Lake.

Acknowledgments

Putting together a guide consisting of such a wide range of topics requires help from many different experts. I was very fortunate in receiving this help and hope that I have interpreted their contributions correctly and clearly.

For providing information, insight, constructive criticism, and encouragement, I would like to thank Bruce Aiken, Jennie Albrinck, Mike Anderson, Michelle Bailey, Jan Balsom, Emma Benenati, Don Bertolette, Andrea Bornemeier, Li Brannfors, Paula Branstner, Ellen Brennan, Steve Bridgehouse, Mike Buchheit, Angelita Bulletts, Jeanne Calhoun, Julie Crawford, Dennis Curtis, Diane Doyle, Charles Drost, Christopher Eaton, Helen Fairley, Pam Frazier, Pete Fulé, Greg Holm, Amy Horn, Martha Kreuger, Don Lago, Mark and Mary McCutcheon, Margaret Moore, Rick Moore, Carol Ogburn, Deidre Paulsen, Tom Pittenger, Jessica Pope, Richard Quartaroli, Wayne Ranney, Donn Reynard, Mandy Reynard, Doug Schwartz, Ellen Seeley, Judy Springer, Amanda Summers, Robin Tellis, Casey Teske, Bill Torres, Scott Thybony, John Vankat, Kate Watters, Marion Werthington, Jim Wessel, Pam Whipple, Stuart Whipple, Catherine Wightman, and Alana Woo.

A special thank you to Claudine Taillac and Susan Tasaki for their remarkable editing skills, and to David Jenney for his creative book design. Also, many thanks to Lulu Santamaria and the rest of the Grand Canyon Conservancy staff for their support of this project.

Any statements of opinion or errors of fact are strictly my own.

Photography Credits

Bruce Aiken 64; Stewart Aitchison 37, 89 bottom, 90 top; Tom Bean 18 top, 54, 57 bottom, 77 top; Chris Brown 53 bottom; Tom Brownold 8; Ron Bohr 86; Mike Buchheit 42; BYU, Harold B. Lee Library 60 top, 87; Michael Collier 95 bottom; Dick Dietrich 84; Michael Fogden Photography 103; Grand Canyon National Park Museum Collection: iv Mike Quinn; 3 Robin Tellis; 4; 9; 16; 18 #5281; 20; 21; 23 Erin Whittaker; 28 #0521; 29 bottom #05498; 31 Mike Quinn; 38 top Brent Riegsecker; 38 bottom #10455; 43 top Mark Lellouch; 43 bottom Mike Quinn; 44 #0253 Mike Quinn; 48 top #87-3462 Mike Quinn; 48 bottom #0081 Mike Quinn; 49 top #05498; 50 top; 50 bottom; 55 bottom; 57 #172290; 58 #05305; 59 #04453; 61; 62 top #00175; 62 bottom #52846; 63 #05988; 65 #06822; 66 #05427; 67 top #0159 Mike Quinn; 67 bottom #66204; 68 #0620 Mike Quinn; 69; 85 #05877; 98 #31347; Grand Canyon–Parashant National Monument 77 bottom, 78 bottom, 81; Paul Gill 91 bottom, 95 top; Bruce Griffin 2; Kenneth Hamblin 30–31, 78–79; Dave Hammaker 5; Jeff Henry 93; Fred Hirschmann 75 top; Brian Gatlin 45, 47, 49 bottom; George H. H. Huey 26, 29 top, 82, 91 top; Liz Hymans 32–33, 89 top; Kerrick James 33; Kaibab National Forest 6 top, 6 bottom, 86; Mike Koopsen 10–11, 17 top, 17 bottom, 22, 34–35, 96; Ann Kramer back cover flap; Chuck Lawson 25, 32; Larry Lindahl front cover top, back cover top, iii top, 13 top, 15, 21 bottom, 25 top, 36, 37 top, 53 top, 55, 83; Natural Light Photography 97; NAU, Cline Library Special Collections and Archives 99 bottom; Sharlot Hall Museum, Prescott, Arizona 73, 75 bottom; Don Singer 46, 52; Derek von Briesen 41; David Welling front cover bottom, back cover bottom, 70–71; Leon Werdinger 94, 99 top; Kathryn Wilde 101; U.S. Geological Survey 1

Contact Information

Arizona Game and Fish Department, Region II Office

3500 S. Lake Mary Road, Flagstaff, AZ 86001
(928) 774-5045
azgfd.com

Dixie/Arizona Strip Interpretive Association

345 East Riverside Drive, St. George, UT 84790-9000
(435) 688-3200
d-asia.org

Glen Canyon National Recreation Area

nps.gov/glca/index.htm

Grand Canyon Conservancy

P.O. Box 399, Grand Canyon, AZ 86023
(800) 858-2808
grandcanyon.org

Grand Canyon National Park

P.O. Box 129, Grand Canyon, AZ 86023
nps.gov/grca

Grand Canyon National Park/North Rim Visitor Center

nps.gov/grca/planyourvisit
(*Includes links to information about lodging and camping*)

Grand Canyon-Parashant National Monument

345 East Riverside Drive, St. George, UT 84790-9000
(435) 688-3200
nps.gov/para

Kaibab Plateau Visitor Center

Jacob Lake, Fredonia, AZ 86022
(928) 643-7298
fs.usda.gov/recarea/kaibab

Kaibab Plateau/North Kaibab Ranger District

P.O. Box 248, Fredonia, AZ 86022
(928) 643-7395
fs.usda.gov/recarea/kaibab

Leave No Trace

P.O. Box 997, Boulder, CO 80306
(303) 442-8222 or (800) 332-4100
LNT.org

Navajo Bridge Interpretive Center

West side of Navajo Bridge on U.S. Highway 89A
(928) 355-2319
www.nps.gov/glca/learn/historyculture/navajobridge.htm

Navajo Nation Parks and Recreation Department

P.O. Box 9000, Window Rock, AZ 86515
(928) 871-6647
navajonationparks.org

Pipe Spring National Monument

HC 65, Box 5, Fredonia, AZ 86022
(928) 643-7105
nps.gov/pisp

Vermilion Cliffs National Monument

345 East Riverside Drive, St. George, UT 84790-9000
(435) 688-3200
blm.gov/visit/vermilion-cliffs

Suggested Reading

Abbott, Lon, Terri Cook. *Hiking the Grand Canyon's Geology*. The Mountaineers Books, 2004.

Aitchison, Stewart. *Grand Canyon: Window of Time*. Sierra Press, 1999.

Anderson, Michael F. *Living at the Edge: Explorers, Exploiters and Settlers of the Grand Canyon Region*. Grand Canyon Association, 1998.

——. *Polishing the Jewel: An Administrative History of Grand Canyon National Park*. Grand Canyon Association, 2000.

Bagley, Will. *Blood of the Prophets: Brigham Young and the Massacre at Mountain Meadows*. University of Oklahoma Press, 2004.

Bailey, Florence Merriam. *Among the Birds in the Grand Canyon Country*. US Government Printing Office, 1939.

Berkowitz, Alan. *Grand Canyon Trail Guide: North Kaibab*. Grand Canyon Association, 1996.

Billingsley, George H., Earle E. Spamer, Dove Menkes. *Quest for the Pillar of Gold: The Mines and Miners of the Grand Canyon.* Grand Canyon Association, 1997.

Brown, Bryan T., Steven W. Carothers, R. Roy Johnson. *Grand Canyon Birds.* University of Arizona Press, 1987.

Coder, Christopher M. *An Introduction to Grand Canyon Prehistory.* Grand Canyon Association, 2000.

Crampton, C. Gregory, ed. *Sharlot Hall on the Arizona Strip.* Northland Press, 1975.

Easton, Robert, Mackenzie Brown. *Lord of the Beasts: The Saga of Buffalo Jones.* University of Arizona Press, 1961.

Grey, Zane. *The Last of the Plainsmen.* The Outing Publishing Company, 1908.

Hall, Joseph G. Linea: *Portrait of a Kaibab Squirrel with Sketches of Other Wildlife on the North Rim of Grand Canyon.* Self-published, 1998.

Hirst, Stephen, contributing ed. *We Call the Canyon Home: American Indians of the Grand Canyon Region.* Grand Canyon Association, 2016.

Holt, Ronald L. *Beneath These Red Cliffs: An Ethnology of the Utah Paiutes.* University of New Mexico Press, 1992.

Houk, Rose. *An Introduction to Grand Canyon Ecology.* Grand Canyon Association, 1996.

Lago, Don. *The Powell Expedition: New Discoveries about John Wesley Powell's 1869 River Journey.* University of Nevada Press, 2018.

Lamb, Susan. *Grand Canyon Wild Life Rim to River.* Grand Canyon Association, 2013.

Leach, Nicky. *Pipe Spring National Monument.* Zion Natural History Association, 1999.

Leavengood, Betty. *Grand Canyon Women: Lives Shaped by Landscape.* Grand Canyon Association, 2014.

Martineau, LaVan. *Southern Paiutes: Legends, Lore, Language, and Lineage.* KC Publications, 1992.

Moore, Margaret M., David W. Huffman. "Tree Encroachment on Meadows of the North Rim, Grand Canyon National Park, Arizona, U.S.A." (2004). *Arctic, Antarctic, and Alpine Research,* 36:4, pp. 474–483.

National Park Service, U.S. Department of the Interior. "Grand Canyon Bison Nativity, Genetics, and Ecology: Looking Forward," Natural Resource Report NPS/NRSS/BRD/NRR—2016/1226.

Pauly, Thomas H. *Zane Grey: His Life, His Adventures, His Women.* University of Illinois Press, 2005.

Powell, James Lawrence. *Grand Canyon: Solving Earth's Grandest Puzzle.* Pearson Education, Inc, 2005.

Price, Edna. *Burro Bill and Me.* Death Valley Natural History Association, 1993.

Price, L. Greer. *An Introduction to Grand Canyon Geology.* Grand Canyon Association, 1999.

Ranney, Wayne. *Carving Grand Canyon: Evidence, Theories, and Mystery.* Grand Canyon Association, 2012.

Reilly, P.T. *Lees Ferry from Mormon Crossing to National Park.* Utah State University Press, 1999.

Rider, Rowland W. as told to Deirdre Paulsen. *The Roll Away Saloon: Cowboy Tales of the Arizona Strip.* Utah State University Press, 1985.

Schmidt, Jeremy. *A Natural History Guide: Grand Canyon National Park.* Houghton Mifflin Company, 1993.

Schwartz, Douglas W. *On the Edge of Splendor: Exploring Grand Canyon's Human Past.* School of American Research, 1989.

Smiley, Francis E., Christian E. Downum, Susan G. Smiley, eds. *The Archaeology of Grand Canyon: Ancient People, Ancient Places.* Grand Canyon Association, 2016.

Stegner, Wallace. *Beyond the Hundredth Meridian: John Wesley Powell and the Second Opening of the West.* Penguin Books, 1954.

Swanson, Frederick H. *Dave Rust: A Life in the Canyons.* University of Utah Press, 2008.

Thybony, Scott. *Official Guide to Hiking Grand Canyon.* Grand Canyon Association, 2005.

Warner, Ted J., ed. *The Domínguez-Escalante Journal: Their Expedition through Colorado, Utah, Arizona, and New Mexico in 1776.* University of Utah Press, 1995.

Index